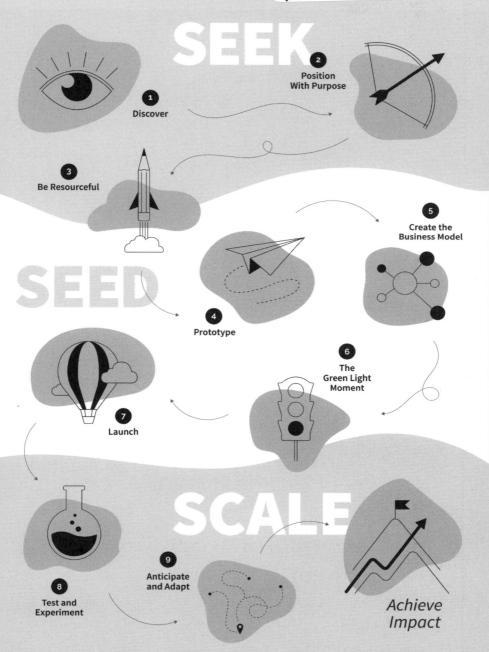

SEEK

1 Discover

2 Position With Purpose

3 Be Resourceful

SEED

4 Prototype

5 Create the Business Model

6 The Green Light Moment

7 Launch

SCALE

8 Test and Experiment

9 Anticipate and Adapt

Achieve Impact

CULTURE

CONNECTIONS

CAPABILITIES

"As a fellow change maker, I've long admired Amy Radin's impact and resilience. In *The Change Maker's Playbook*, she offers a practical guide to getting to the other side of change in a way that creates value and meaning. An important resource for anyone looking to innovate better."

—Beth Comstock, author of *Imagine It Forward* and former Vice Chair, GE

"What businesses need today is change makers: driven leaders who turn market disruption into innovation opportunities, creating real impact and value. If you're up for this, Amy Radin's fearlessly focused and practical book is your next must-read."

—David Rogers, Columbia Business School faculty and best-selling author of *The Digital Transformation Playbook*

"Seek. Seed. Scale. Amy Radin's formula for innovation is uncommonly clear. The true lesson woven throughout the book is that it all begins and ends with culture, an important lesson for organizations of every size."

—Ajay Banga, President and Chief Executive Officer, Mastercard

"Innovation is clearly a MUST but never comes easily. Thanks to *The Change Maker's Playbook*, we now have a practical, actionable guide to help tackle the non-negotiable task of delivering value through innovation."

—Emma Weisberg, Head of Global Business Marketing, Waze

"This book has become my team's manifesto. Radin inspires you to keep the momentum while laying out the steps to move through the inevitable resistance you'll face. This is the book for teams with a bold agenda."

—Dave Edelman, Chief Marketing Officer, Aetna

"An indispensable guide for marketers and those who want to truly deliver better products and experiences for their customers, not just talk about it. In her accessible and relatable way, Radin lays out the path for finding and delivering innovation essential to brand impact."
—Lewis Gersh, Founder and CEO,
PebblePost

"So much of innovation focuses on developing and testing breakthrough ideas. Yet, the vast majority of these ideas fail to be adopted. Amy Radin not only focuses on the generation of innovative ideas (seeking), but also the process of shepherding those ideas through organizational hurdles (seeding), and become drivers of real organizational performance (scaling). Executives who find themselves in an increasingly fast-paced and unpredictable world would be well advised to seek counsel in *The Change Maker's Playbook*."
—Michael Wade, Cisco Chair in Digital
Business Transformation, Professor of
Innovation and Strategy, IMD

"Radin's Seek, Seed, Scale framework should be in the workspace of any leader who wants to create sustainable franchises and shape the future (and not be undone by the forces at play in today's world)."
—Ashok Vaswani, CEO, Barclays UK

THE
CHANGE MAKER'S
PLAYBOOK

HOW TO SEEK, SEED AND SCALE
INNOVATION IN ANY COMPANY

AMY J. RADIN

City Point Press

City Point Press
286 Curtis Avenue
Stratford, CT 06615
www.citypointpress.com

ISBN: 978-1-947951-06-8
eBook ISBN: 978-1-947951-07-5

Cover and book design by Barbara Aronica Buck
Cover illustration from iStock.com/-1001-
Iconography by Jessica Berardi for Pilgrim
Figures on pages 174–175 are adapted from originals created by Geoff Chellis, Expedia Consulting Group
Figure on page 239 is adapted from an original created by Donna Peeples, Motivated, Inc.

Manufactured in Canada

CONTENTS

FOREWORD

For at least a dozen years before I finally met her, I heard rumors of Amy Radin. As a partner at Diamond Management & Technology Consultants, where we pioneered the idea of digital strategy in the mid-1990s, I made it my business to know as many leading innovators as possible, and Amy's name kept surfacing among my partners because of the work she was doing, first at Citigroup and then at E*Trade.

Before joining Diamond, I spent seventeen years majoring in innovation as an editor and reporter at the *Wall Street Journal*, mostly covering technology. My first book, *Big Blues: The Unmaking of IBM*, a best seller about IBM's near-death experience, which I published in 1993, hit what has become the prime innovation theme for me and for much of the business world ever since: What happens when a major company doesn't adapt quickly enough to step-changes in digital technology? My partners and I later explored that theme at Diamond, where we helped clients go on the offensive by unleashing "killer apps." We struck a nerve directly enough that *Context,* the small-circulation magazine I developed and edited for Diamond, was a finalist in 2000 for the National Magazine Award for General Excellence.

The focus on separating innovation winners from losers persisted when I left Diamond and went out on my own, pursuing the mantra, "Smart people, interesting projects." Those people and projects eventually connected me with Amy.

Jim Collins has done great research into what drives corporate successes for his books *Built to Last* and *Good to Great*, but I realized around 2005 that no one had taken a systematic look at failures. And you have to understand both sides of the equation, right? You not only have to know what to do; you have to see where the land mines are, to understand what *not* to do. Chunka Mui and I got our old friends at Diamond to lend us twenty researchers over the course of two years to look at 2,500 failures. We turned the research into a book, *Billion Dollar Lessons: How to Learn From the Most Inexcusable Business Failures of the Last 25 Years*, which drew rave reviews, including from the *WSJ*. Amid all the great research (really . . . and it's still in print), the fundamental insight of the book was that nearly half of the failures we studied stemmed from ideas that were obviously flawed, but that weren't blocked because internal dynamics glossed over the problems. What was needed was a devil's advocate who would make sure that all assumptions were brought to the surface and that all uncomfortable questions were asked. That insight led us to work with some of the world's top strategists, and to several fascinating consulting engagements with Chunka, as the Devil's Advocate Group. Eventually, the "smart people and interesting projects" mantra brought me to insurance, one of the four areas that we identified a few years ago as still virgin territory for digital disruption. (The others were government, higher education, and medicine.)

By this point, Amy had made her way to insurance, too, as chief marketing officer for AXA, following her senior operating role at Citi and innovation role at E*Trade. At a time when insurance had yet to catch the "insurtech" fever that has taken hold over the past couple of years, she shone as one of the very few lights in the firmament. I had become the editor-in-chief of Insurance Thought Leadership, a startup publishing platform trying to drive innovation in risk management and insurance, and I decided I finally had to meet Amy. She graciously agreed, and, over coffee at the Grand Hyatt in New York City, we had a meeting of the minds. Chunka and I had summarized our approach to innovation as "Think big, start small, and learn fast." Amy had landed in a similar spot (with the terms Seeking, Seeding, and Scaling, as you'll see in this book). Crucially, she also supplements her thinking with a huge amount of practical experience, actually getting stuff done inside big organizations. As a result, she understands that, as much as we might wish otherwise, innovation isn't linear; the process needs to jump, double back, do loop-the-loops, iterate, repeat, whatever . . . but within strict enough parameters that you stay focused on the goal and eventually get there.

Amy agreed to become part of the ITL Advisory Board, so I've had the excuse to pick her brain for more than three years now, and to watch as she has expanded her repertoire considerably by investing in and advising many startups, beyond mine. She was more than worth the wait.

She is exceptionally smart and insightful and down-to-earth. I developed a world-class B.S. detector during my days at the *WSJ*, and I promise that Amy is as straightforward as they come. I'm delighted that she's chosen to share her experience and her insights more broadly in this book. I think you'll learn a lot. I certainly did.

Enjoy.

Paul B. Carroll
Roseville, CA

INTRODUCTION

Innovation can be polarizing. It conjures up coolness and threat, inevitability and unpredictability, attraction and avoidance. Innovation is essential, yet fails more often than it succeeds.

My reaction to a particular, recent innovation reported in local press was to smile. The New York City Metropolitan Transit Authority announced the rollout of contactless payments technology in the New York City transit system—the world's largest commuter transportation infrastructure. Why my reaction? Back in 2006, I was a member of the team that implemented the Lexington Avenue Subway Trial—one of the first such pilots in the world. We chose a tough but fertile proving ground by focusing on the commuter experience in a huge market with among the longest, and at times most challenging, trips back and forth to work. The pilot was built in a three-way partnership between Citi, Mastercard, and the transit authority. It "failed"—that is, if you define failure as not getting the green light to scale.

When such pilots don't immediately generate miracle results, the hindsight analyses are easy. We were too early by over a decade. We had the wrong device—a cool but nonetheless limited-use, expensive "fob" that attached to users' key rings. The business model was built only for bank account holders. And internal resistance in the pre-millennial economy was formidable. But now, with contactless payments becoming ubiquitous, the important rearview mirror lesson is how much better it is to harvest learning and decide next moves to grab a market lead, than to deem such experiments as one-and-done events.

The Subway Trial is just one story, with one set of lessons. This book gives change makers in any organization dozens of hands-on ways to learn from real experiences, so they can take insights about market needs from napkin back to viable businesses that deliver impact.

In my first career I held a series of executive-level marketing, digital, and innovation roles at big brands. Seeing the possibilities to effect greater change, I launched a new career helping leaders do what needed to get done to move businesses forward. My passion became working with change makers to create new value and growth amidst the rapid change and rising complexity that is everywhere. My board, advisory, and consulting work led to research with dozens of founders, investors, corporate innovators, and thought leaders. I decided to write *The Change Maker's Playbook*, bringing together these remarkable individuals' experiences, along with my own, to benefit and inspire others.

This book is for leaders who want to solve unmet market needs. These people don't just have ideas. They feel commitment and have a sense of purpose to create new forms of value and growth of benefit to employees, customers, partners, and shareholders. They want to move with urgency, speeding progress by learning from others' experiences.

The recommendations included throughout have all been tried out in diverse organizations, from global brands to garage-based startups, not-for-profits and privately held high-growth companies. Every recommendation comes from people whose collective experiences will resonate in any company, in any size, sector, or life stage. The common ingredient is that within these organizations there is a change maker who has set out to reinvent products and services or entire businesses, to turn unsolved market problems into opportunities.

The stories of successful entrepreneurs, corporate innovators, investors, government and not-for-profit leaders, and thinkers have been organized in an accessible framework. The framework is rooted in practice, and proven by innovation operators. It does not stop at theory, strategic insights, or ideas. It is packed with tactics that work. That is why this book is the practical guide and indispensable resource for any change maker to keep close at hand. The content's user-friendly format will help readers take techniques straight into any live innovation setting. The *Playbook* is organized into three parts according to the Seek, Seed, and Scale framework.

PART I, SEEKING, starts with what it means to discover insights into problems and define purpose to drive value and growth. Too many aspiring innovators jump to create the perfect product for themselves. Maybe they are under pressure to hit a forecast and are bound by internal perspectives. Reality check: Is there a big and deep enough problem in the market, and is there commitment and purpose from the get-go? This section establishes how to find and define what to build, identifying the change maker mindset that will make the difference through all elements of the framework.

PART II, SEEDING, tackles the skills, tools, leadership, and capabilities that get concepts to take hold by testing for market interest and feedback. Seeding conditions are different for young, fragile concepts than for those of mature businesses. Seeding requires iteration, to get the right mix of elements. Rough concepts must prove they can be viable, and solve real problems for a scale audience. They are best proven and refined by engaging users in prototypes of how the solution is envisioned to work.

PART III, SCALING, focuses on the last three steps of the framework, and takes great ideas toward the ranks of sustainable businesses, assuring vitality through the future forces of change. *Launch* spans the days or weeks or months surrounding the "go live" moment. Presented sequentially, but built-in to *Launch*, are *Testing and Experimenting*.

Finally, the framework ends with new beginnings: *Anticipating and Adapting*. However great the results, no one can afford to sit still and ignore the reality of future reinvention.

Scaling does not just mean doing everything in a bigger version of what's happened until now. Scaling is a function of what you've been doing *bigger*, what you've been doing *adapted*, and *whole new* activities, choices, and relationships. Scaling means a new trajectory. As such, it requires shifts in mindset, approach, skills, and how resources are used.

Each *Playbook* chapter explains and animates:

➤ **What needs to happen?** Stories highlight the experiences of change makers—how they made decisions and faced down challenges. These are deliberately not celebrities' stories. They are the stories of real people with the sense of purpose and commitment to achieve opportunities that began as grains of ideas or observations and evolved, generating tangible results.

➤ **What are the steps to get there?** Each chapter includes a section called "The Three Cs." These are Capabilities, Connections, and Culture, the methods and mindset for moving the book's content from theory to action to results. Processes, templates, tools, checklists, and other tactics are provided to enable action.

➤ **What can be taken away and applied from each chapter?** A chapter summary wraps up each element of the framework, and serves as a reference list and reminder.

The *Playbook* is not intended to portray innovation as linear, predictably paced or methodically timed. Innovation is dynamic, iterative, and even messy—particularly when viewed according to how businesses used to work. Innovation shifts back, forth, and sideways, and does not look the same twice. What is covered through the framework might happen in weeks, months or years. Steps are uneven, loaded with ambiguity. Progress requires purpose, commitment, new methods, intense execution, and also takes guesswork and judgment in the absence of certainty and hard data. Luck plays a role.

These dynamics are the norm to create an offering, or reshape existing products and services. Repetition of the past is not the recipe. There is no set recipe.

Market problems are tougher than ever to solve well and at scale. To change makers, this means more innovation opportunity. Capabilities are out there, to be applied toward the needs spawned by trends. More data may hold answers to pressing problems. Generational shifts in attitudes and values are opening up opportunities, demographic change is creating demand, and social media and new channel technologies are widening access.

Take inspiration, execute, and get results by…

➤ Learning from dozens of successful change makers: the entrepreneurs, corporate innovators, investors, and thought leaders who participated in the research upon which this book is based;

➤ Taking advantage of a user-friendly, tested, and shareable toolkit that you can bookmark, highlight, click on, and keep close at hand;

➤ Moving from framework to real world, applying practical methods to accomplish your innovation aspirations.

Change makers are few in number, and are worthy of encouragement and support. They want to create and deliver value, bring together teams to solve big problems, seize opportunities, and make a difference. Treading water is not an option for them. They want to succeed for themselves, their communities, friends and loved ones, and for the broader stakeholder ecosystem. Theirs are hard-won achievements.

Success is happening for those who adopt a new mindset, tactics, and commitment, and who establish their purpose. Following the old script won't work.

If you see a career runway in front of you, want to commit to innovate with the goal of creating value and growth for stakeholders, and to serve customers by understanding and solving their problems, you will find value in this book. If you are marking time to jump ship, talking the talk about innovation while your head and heart are not walking the walk, this book will make little sense. Purpose-driven leaders, this book is for you. Financial engineers and valuation hypesters, sorry, this book cannot help.

The Change Maker's Playbook will provide guidance to get from the napkin-back idea to tangible impacts.

Are you ready to be a change maker?

Read on.

PART I:

SEEKING

"We have two ears and
one mouth so we can listen twice
as much as we speak."

Attributed to Epictetus,
Greek Philosopher, b 55 d 135

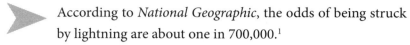According to *National Geographic*, the odds of being struck by lightning are about one in 700,000.[1]

As an educated guess, the odds that an amazing innovation will simply occur to you, show up in your inbox, or come as a result of scraping trends from secondary source materials are also extraordinarily low.

To create innovation, you have to take action. There is no fixed formula. But a no-downside starting point is to listen—both to your inner voice, and to the sources of useful feedback in your surroundings. Some sources are obvious. Many are not.

Part I, *Seeking*, presents stories, advice and tools to help change makers be better at proactively listening for market insights, then blend them together to help:

> ➤ Define purpose that is important enough to earn your commitment;

> ➤ Identify the big market problems that you can solve within your business context;

> ➤ Connect your sense of purpose with the big problems;

> ➤ Take steps to convert your commitment into strategy and action;

> ➤ Shape solutions by tapping into your creativity, network, and know-how to prove value and growth potential, even when resources seem limited.

There is no set timeline, but those who act with speed and urgency gain the advantage. What most matters now is to create the foundation. That is where listening, insight, purpose, and commitment come into play. Why? The first chapters of this *Playbook* connect the dots between these elements and achieving results. Quite simply: You are setting yourself up to go after market opportunity. And you care enough about the goal to face down the many challenges ahead.

You may have a jumpstart with answers informed by life experiences. Founders like to share the stories of how and why their ventures began with a problem they personally experienced or saw in others, and cared about enough to solve even against the immense odds of ever succeeding.

Seeking behaviors come first, and benefit all aspects of the framework. The three chapters of Part I address:

➤ **Discovery.** Learning about users and buyers by exploring and synthesizing what you find in actionable insights.

➤ **Purpose, passion, promise, and positioning.** Knowing what you are committed to, defining a solution to a deep and wide problem, and establishing how to represent your purpose and promise in the market.

➤ **Resourcefulness.** A figure-out-whatever-it-will-take attitude and behaviors, knowing that money, time, and people resources will always be tight.

As you head off to explore, observe behavior and be attentive to nonverbal signals and cues. Find the truths that won't be spoken. Sometimes the feedback is implicit in a question posed to you. Sometimes the best prompt to learn more about whether a user values a prototype is to say nothing—to make space for insight with a pause.

Set yourself up to innovate by being open—and as a result, allow for possibilities.

CHAPTER 1:
Discovering Real Needs

Making an effort to listen—to hear, observe, and understand people—will make you a great discoverer. Proactive learners who are accepting, curious, and inquiring are good listeners. Who do you think listens well? Think about why—what listening behaviors can you adopt?

Discoverers want to understand where people are coming from: their backgrounds and environment, motivations and emotions. Discoverers back away from being in "I already know it" mode. They collaborate. They pursue dialogue, not interrogation. For those who are curious, discovery is fun.

Greg Burns, executive coach and Citi's former chief learning officer, believes anyone can improve their listening and discovery abilities. He says, "It all starts with mindfulness, being in the moment, being able to turn your brain off and really focus on the other person."[2]

This chapter investigates how to be a discoverer, and further, how and when to turn discovery into learning that will set you off to define value and growth concepts.

People buy painkillers, not vitamins

Change makers use proven methods to get insights about people and what innovations will address their needs.

Needs are rational: I need food because I am hungry; by the way, I prefer that it tastes good. And, it has to be affordable and sold where I shop. Product features meet rational aspects of needs. Needs are also emotional and influenced by values: I'm a mom, and after a long day, I want to put a healthy, tasty dinner on the table to promote good family habits.

Product features address functional needs, but are often limited to the basics. Truly innovative solutions go beyond rational needs, and connect with emotional needs and values. Emotional connection doesn't mean soft-edged photography, or other communications clichés. Emotional needs may not be terribly profound. They are waiting to be solved within life's day-to-day irritants and inconveniences.

A fellow innovator once said, "People buy pain killers, not vitamins." Living as we do with so much complexity, relief from life's hassles alone can earn attention and commitment to a brand. Take, for example, ketchup.

Do you buy ketchup? Does your ketchup bottle sit right side up or upside down? Heinz ketchup dates back to 1876. In 2002, Heinz's business goal was to grow sales. Discovery led to a user problem: the hassle involved in getting the last bit of ketchup out of the bottle. Users reportedly jammed knives down the bottles, or shook bottles hard only to be squirted with a watery mess, or tried balancing the right-side-up bottle upside down (my favorite technique). Given the long narrow neck and wide bottom, that is a tough act.

Heinz responded by introducing the inverted ketchup bottle, applying a package design first invented for shampoo. Providing a better alternative to user workarounds revolutionized a 150-year-old product.

Heinz grew at three times the market rate within a year of this new-to-category innovation.[3]

Takeaways:

➤ Listening includes observing user behavior—the source of insights beyond what people might reveal in conversation.

➤ The more interesting problems to solve are those that connect to emotional needs, but they don't need to be anything fancy. Alleviating small daily hassles earns customer loyalty and pricing, margin, and distribution advantages.

How to be a better listener:

➤ An open mind—a blank slate—makes it easier to recognize opportunity. The more filters, the more potential to miss the big problem waiting to be solved. Aim your category knowledge to areas that leverage your knowledge, but don't allow knowing too much to become a disadvantage. You carry biases as a consequence of your expertise.

➤ A wide definition of potential users can lead to surprising opportunities. But execution benefits from a well-defined audience. Distribution systems may be fragmented, so identifying common behavior patterns among the big-enough populations will pay off. Not sure? There will be opportunities to test. The best segments may not yet be clear. Anticipate creating a knowledge inventory to keep track of segmentation ideas. Look for more on segmentation in Chapter 8, *Testing and Experimenting*.

➤ Take a deliberate approach to deciding from whom to seek insights. Include not just users, but also influencers, decision makers, and even people whose experiences in different markets or categories offer learning. For example, my teams in payments saw that people's habits around managing money and health have much in common. Learning about dieting strategies stimulated ideas for financial services product experiences, and helped us break away from incremental, easily copied products.

➤ Avoid sources bound to confirm what you already believe. Move further afield. There is no better time to explore beyond the familiar than now.

Are you simply solving your own problem?

What's great about jumping into a problem that stems from one's own experience is the deep understanding and passion to fix something that is bothering you.

The founder solving their own problem has to avoid building the perfect solution for their personal-use case, only to find they are not solving a problem of interest to many other people.

The corporate innovator may be on a team that does not include product users. They must account for their own personal detachment from what it is like to have a particular problem. They have the added responsibility of selling up the ladder, to executive team or board members removed from the daily realities of customers, and focused more on the internal demands of a grown-up company facing disruption.

Creating momentum to pursue innovation takes a lot of energy, commitment, and belief. Even if you need just a small amount of cash to get going, you may be depleting a department budget, negotiating with colleagues to depart with theirs, or using limited political capital to advocate for something that has not been done before. If you are a founder, you may be emptying your own savings or asking friends and family to trust you with theirs.

Users, buyers, and payers all matter

Back to household ketchup consumption, different family members each have an influence on which bottle of ketchup will be pulled off the supermarket shelf. Heads of household pay for the item, but family members all around the table are users. Perhaps a caregiver or relative handles grocery shopping. It's important to understand the roles each member of the influence group plays, early on, to inform product priorities. Start to anticipate the complete experience.

Like tens of millions of other households, my family has a Netflix subscription. I am the *payer*: the subscription is a recurring charge to my credit card. My daughter is the *user*: after homework is done, she tunes in. Her friends send texts to each other about the latest content, and are all *influencers* of entertainment choices. Our childcare provider may be the *buyer*, monitoring the clock, the homework progress, and the weekly screen time tally. When my husband and I are not home, she gets to be gatekeeper, saying yes or no to my daughter's pleading for relief from the never-ending boredom of digital-age, preadolescent, suburban life.

The user/buyer/payer/influencer model applies to business-to-consumer (B2C), business-to-business (B2B), and business-to-business-to-consumer (B2B2C) use cases. The constellation of players varies.

Say I'm the founder of a startup selling a bookkeeping solution to Main Street retailers. Unlike the Netflix example, where roles are each played by different people, in this example the buyer and payer are likely one and the same—the business owner. The user may also be the owner, or could be an on-site employee or remote contractor. The influencers could be diverse—including authoritative bloggers writing product reviews, or trusted neighborhood retailers.

At a global life insurance carrier, I led a team that proved out this model for the purchase of a big-ticket, complex product sold through intermediaries.

A couple has a child, triggering a conversation about life insurance. The parents influence each other, and decide to consult other influencers, including favorite online sources for personal financial information, or maybe college buddies. Wanting to understand products not (yet) available online, they call upon an adviser, who brings in yet another influencer, a broker. The couple ultimately decides. They are both buyer and payer. Who is the user? Well, the parents are receiving and paying for the emotional value of peace of mind, and may realize the rational value of tapping into a policy's cash value. Other users are those named as beneficiaries.

Figuring out the roles of user, buyer, payer, and influencer for emerging use cases is a great way to organize insights to be productive. This model:

> ➤ Helps home in on feature, positioning, and experience priorities;

> ➤ Shrinks an unwieldy list of product features and nixes the ones you may have fallen in love with, but have turned out to be unimportant;

> ➤ Gets well beyond demographics, which are interesting but way too superficial, to reveal what you need to know about the people you want to serve;

➤ Puts the problem and solutions into the context of people's lives;

➤ Zeroes in on the behaviors that affect how people make decisions to buy, producing downstream benefits for go-to-market activities.

The user/buyer/payer/influencer model is one that's both useful and easy to apply. Try it out as a mental model or in writing, completed on your own or with colleagues. Begin with users. Ultimately what matters is to map all members of the system and to understand how they affect each other's decisions. A sample format is included later in this chapter, in the Three Cs section.

What people do trumps what they say

Customer journey mapping has become a mini-industry all its own. There is plenty of attention, including lip service, paid to the customer journey. Most brands circumscribe the definition around engagement with their own products or channels. From the perspective of users and buyers, though, the journey begins at the moment they realize they have a need, through researching, buying, and post-purchase usage, payment, and servicing.

The value of customer journey mapping is threefold. It can:

➤ Find the actionable business levers of user, buyer, payer, and influencer behavior;

➤ Ferret out problems occurring along the journey that are core to your solution, or that might *be* the solution;

➤ Identify actionable segmentation strategies to apply to media, messaging, and positioning decisions later on.

Create the best customer journey framework by focusing on phases:

➤ **Awareness.** How people become aware of unmet needs.

➤ **Investigation.** How those who gain awareness then go about figuring out what to do. Often they pursue a favorite option— they do nothing. Maybe they ask friends or family, go online to search for solutions, read an article, or speak with an expert. Sometimes they don't become aware until presented with a solution. (Did any of us *know* we had to have an iPhone?)

➤ **Deciding.** How do people decide what to buy? Is it what Amazon stocks or what is on sale at the supermarket? Or are choices serendipitous? Is an adviser recommending a product? Do people decide in consultation with a partner? Is there a chain of approval that drives the decision?

➤ **After the purchase.** What happens post-purchase? More purchases of the same? Or the possibilities of a trade-up, extension, warranty activation, breakdown, defect, claim, or return?

See if you can identify different behavior patterns that spark ideas about segments.

The most effective way to figure out the customer journey is through a combination of observing and getting inside user and buyer thought processes, to see how choices are made and behaviors influenced at each step.

A helpful line of questioning starts with just a few questions:

1. What did you do? And then what? And then what?

2. What made you think to do that? What else? And what else?

Down the road, journey specifics can be fleshed out in more detail, refined, and applied to marketing, product, servicing, and other elements of execution.

Sometimes only a crisis can illuminate discovery

How can you invest efforts in discovery if you operate inside a culture that doesn't like ambiguity and perceives the work of the change maker as too messy? A good discovery raises questions, not just provides answers.

Sometimes, change only comes when an urgent situation arises demanding something new happen, especially in a rooted culture, and especially one where the company has a legacy of achievement.

In a historically successful place, running around shouting that the sky is falling will backfire. And even providing indisputable evidence won't guarantee buy-in. Sponsorship, credibility, influence, and relationships matter to win others over to change—the greater the change in direction, the tougher the shift.

Two pieces of advice, both assuming commitment to purpose:

1. Focus others on the possibilities of what could be. Showing not just passion, but well thought-through execution, even at this early stage, helps win sponsorship and build a circle of supporters.

2. Use your network to find a mentor from whom you can learn the tricks of remaining true to your vision and the steps necessary to deliver.

A crisis may have to happen to mobilize a team to listen and act.

Bill Unrue was CEO of Anonymizer, an Internet privacy and online identity management business, when all fundraising options dried up after the Internet bubble burst in 2000.

"We couldn't get any VC money, so we had to earn our way out. We had to slow down and listen to the customer," Bill said.[4] He shared the team's realization that paying attention to customer signals would define the company's future. "Extinction has a way of focusing the mind. The only path for us was to listen to the customer to find what we could monetize." The company ultimately achieved a good exit, fueled by customer insight that led management to reset priorities and rethink the highest potential sources of revenue aligned with their purpose.

Steal shamelessly

Never underestimate the ability to get great customer insights on a low (or no) budget. "Steal shamelessly," a global CEO once said to me. Go for good-enough do-it-yourself ways to make progress. How to make high-quality discovery progress:

> ➤ Use your natural abilities to hear, see, smell, and taste. Self-assess how effectively you are putting your senses to work. Are you so absorbed in daily blocking and tackling that you aren't paying attention to what's not on your to-do list? Pick a handful of people who know you well enough to offer useful feedback on how well you listen. Practice getting better. A simple

start to improve: stop constructing in your head what you plan to say next while others are speaking.

➤ "Person on the street" interviews are a time-tested way to find broad insights. This means walking up to people on the street. Or, if you are seeking insights from a defined segment, identify people who fit the profile by looking first within your network. Try conducting five or ten half-hour interviews. Ask open-ended questions outlined in advance. Be ready to let the other person take the discussion in new directions that may not have occurred to you. A sample discussion guide is included at the end of this chapter in the Three Cs section.

➤ If practical, ask a few people to let you come by and hang out to observe a day or even a few hours in their lives. While companies with budgets hire consultants to lead this sort of ethnographic research, a thoughtful do-it-yourself approach can be good enough for starters. I still recall an in-home interview with a middle-class couple, a few years after the start of the financial crisis. If I had only the benefit of their narrative, I would have believed the family was on a steady savings, spending, and budgeting path. But the grocery-store bag in the corner of the dining room, overflowing with unopened statements, told a different story.

Insights don't just come from research methods. Raja Rajamannar is Mastercard's chief marketing and communications officer and president of its Healthcare business division. Raja is always on the lookout for new insight and ideas to drive value and growth. He credits three-quarters of the ideas his team pursues to sources outside the company.

"I read every single email I get, because even if I have to go through ten thousand emails to find one great idea, the time invested is worthwhile."[5]

Raja's other tactics:

➤ Attending industry forums and events;

➤ Running innovation challenges inside the organization;

➤ Looking beyond one's own sector for translatable ideas.

Don't just bet on your own horse

Be sensitive to the risks of do-it-yourself. Discovery requires an open mind. The common trap is to seek customer feedback as validation. Entrepreneurs fall in love with their ideas, and then listen for the answers they preferred all along. So do corporate teams under pressure to generate revenue. Or, in this age of agile product development, the focus ends up on the offering itself, and not the broader context of the customer journey.

That is why, budget permitting, whether for entrepreneur or corporate innovator, there is value in having a third party with no stake in the outcome assisting in discovery. This is not to say throw discovery over the fence. It's risky to say: "I'll read the report when it comes back from the field."

Think about discovery as co-development with users.

Discovery expert Matt Foley is an entrepreneur-in-residence at the High Tech Rochester (HTR) accelerator. Matt built and exited PluggedIn, which became a building block for the insights capability of global public relations and marketing consultancy Edelman.

Matt's perspective applies to any change maker: "I've gone out and sat with entrepreneurs in conversations they are having with customers, and in the end we hear completely different things. I don't have a horse in the race, so I hear things differently. Usually they just hear the positives. The challenge is when you don't have money to hire an expert. What I advise: go into 'mixed mode.' Get together with customers. If your focus is B2B, go to their offices and see their environment. In any case, take a contextual approach."[6]

He says, "People are often too nice to entrepreneurs. Sometimes I'll have someone say to me, 'I have a great idea, but I can't find anyone to talk to me about it.' Well, if you aren't able to find a few people to talk to just to get feedback, you are going to have a helluva time selling it to lots of others down the road."

Matt recommends setting up a customer advisory panel to generate ongoing insights and pay adequate attention to changes in the market. Getting potential customers engaged in discovery is by itself a step toward market validation. It is not difficult to assemble a group of people who will offer opinions and share their stories. To get the right people:

➤ Be precise about whom you recruit;

➤ Create incentives for participation and candor;

➤ Avoid disincentives that bring in the wrong people or encourage spin;

➤ Be prepared, so everyone's time is respected.

Erasmus said, "In the land of the blind,
the one-eyed man is king"[7]

Cofounder of the startup Kavyar, Sean Charles, uses discovery methods to connect artists with publishing opportunities in photography, fashion, beauty, modeling, and the arts.

His motivation to launch was to solve a problem in his own fashion business. "I was always frustrated with not being able to find photographers and other creative talent. I had the clients, I had the work, and I had the money to hire, but I was limited to the creative talent within my own network."[8]

Sean says, "I got together with two other developers to build the software. We did what a lot of other startups did: we went into a cave for several months to design and build until we had something perfect. We had a false presumption of what a company like Apple might do: develop and release. Our thinking was, 'We know what to do, we will build a better version of what is out there and it will take the world by storm.'"

That was not exactly what happened in Version 1.0. So the team sought guidance from a friend who recommended HTR's Launchpad program. As a member of Launchpad, Kavyar had the good luck to work with Matt Foley. By then, Sean was ready to buy into Matt's recommendations on how to get user insights, and the value of the time and effort to do so.

What value did the Kavyar team's insights efforts deliver?

➤ Priority features stood out more clearly, and nice-to-haves were dropped.

➤ One non-obvious but important insight emerged: The top challenge for up-and-coming creative professionals was they had to do it all—to find paying projects, deliver the work, and promote their portfolios.

➤ As a result, up-and-comers were forced to spend 80 percent of their workdays doing stuff they hated. They were being taken away from projects they loved, and for which they were paid, by administrative tasks.

So the big problem turned out to be that, to be compensated as a creative, it was better to be good at the 80 percent, but to shrink that effort to as little time as possible. Kavyar refined its focus: to compress the 80 percent by automating and standardizing the tedious but essential tasks that took creative people away from their passion to create.

The team's discovery learning:

➤ **Determine the who's and how's of participation.** Be clear on the target, and seek insights from people who fit the profile. Offering inappropriate recruiting incentives biases results, e.g., free product access induces trial, but skews feedback.

➤ **Use your network for recruiting.** Kavyar wanted to get onto the calendars of agency executives, who are notoriously busy people. Sean says, "How we ended up doing it was key. We started to ask friends, 'Do you know anybody…?' We soon got a hit, then three additional referrals from that first meeting. Each referral got an email with the subject line: 'Referral From …,' and they each led to another interview. Suddenly, we were talking to everyone."

➤ **Do not assume that being a subject-matter expert means you understand users and buyers.** Sean says, "If you have domain expertise, that's great, but you probably don't know as much as you think you do. Authenticate by collaborating with the people you want to serve."

This may all sound terribly obvious (as so much of life does, in hindsight). But so many innovation seekers under-invest in discovery. You can win by being the one-eyed person in the valley of the blind.

Measure progress: Take the 1 percent test

Productive discovery can be a reality check on preliminary solution and business model assumptions. A good set of observations or interviews, complemented by a bit of secondary research, can yield early hypotheses about market segments, including size and characteristics, wherewithal to pay, and customer journey.

To see whether this is so, take a back-of-the-envelope "1 percent test."

1. Use whatever rough data is on hand to estimate the total market size—whether that is number of people or units in the market, or the total value of purchases.

2. Multiply by 1 percent.

3. If the answer is big enough, that's a good, albeit extremely crude, indicator that what you are pursuing could be worth pursuing based on the size of the opportunity.

One percent of the market may not mean "success." This is a sanity check that lets you say, "Well, if we achieve one percent share, we have traction and can be viable," so it's worth putting in more effort. Just don't play the "fun with spreadsheets" game and start to tell yourself the business will be huge at 1 percent, which is a big number to hit from a standing start. Bottoms-up analysis will be required, as will balancing of expectations.

The 1 percent test will be used later, too. It's a handy tool when good enough is good enough.

THE THREE Cs FOR DISCOVERING REAL PROBLEMS THAT MATTER

Capabilities

User/buyer/payer/influencer assessment

Use this matrix, or adapt it to be your own, as you gather insights about users, buyers, payers, and influencers.

The sample template is completed based on a hypothetical example, a B2B software purchase, to show how the method works for another type of use case. Don't kid yourself. Personal emotional values frame B2B decisions along with professional motivations and the political considerations that exist in any organization.

Imagine, in this case, the buyer heads decision analytics as a member of a big-company marketing team, and is selecting software.

	USER	BUYER	PAYER	INFLUENCER
Who are they? (Describe in as many dimensions as possible)	Multiple team members with knowledge of statistics, who will be assessing marketing program results and advancing modeling tools for colleagues across the team.	The head of decision analytics, who will lead the process to assess options, coordinate with procurement, CFO, and others, and ensure the software is implemented and used. They will be an ongoing point of contact with vendor.	The chief marketing officer, to whom the buyer will present their recommendation, and whose "blessing" is necessary to close the deal.	The CFO, whose buy-in the CMO finds desirable, as this decision will instigate change and lead to decisions and recommendations affecting financials.
What are their motivations and interrelationships relative to the user problem?	Relationships: team head, peer analyst team members, internal clients on assigned projects, implementation team members. All are motivated by ease of use.	Relationships: technical experts in data analytics, operations, IT, internal clients. Motivators are personal success and happy colleagues.	Relationships: agency, other vendors, IT, other CMOs, marketing, line management, sales head—a complex network. Motivators: Prove results, juggle multiple perspectives.	Relationships are with rest of C-suite, CEO, and BOD, as well as to external shareholder community. Motivation: Prove that results satisfy employee needs.

	USER	BUYER	PAYER	INFLUENCER
What are their rational needs relative to the problem?	On time, accurate, advanced methods to prove program performance.	Project delivery, good pacing with emerging requirements.	Demonstrating marketing ROI and being in step with C-suites' perception of digital requirements.	Predictable earnings, risk management.
Emotional needs and values?[9]	Accomplishment, recognition, autonomy, truth.	Control, recognition, family security.	Recognition, accomplishment, family security.	Control, appearance, accomplishment.
What is their role at each stage of the customer journey? How do they affect preferences, choices, the journey itself?	Give feedback on usability, relevance, and feasibility. Accountable to head of team.	Recommend best option to purchase, negotiate deal. Accountable to CMO and to analytics team.	Supports the decision to rest of organization—peers and C-suite; troubleshoots issues.	Represents the outputs as they tie into overall financial performance reporting. Gets behind the investment, including ongoing.

Two active listening exercises

1. Cultivate focus as a daily habit

- **Ask yourself:** "How am I doing today?"
- **Get centered.** This means calm your emotions, and slow your mind and breathing to a point where you can sense what is going on around and within. It's a combined feeling of being very alert, and very relaxed at the same time.
- **Focus.** Feeling cynical? Tell yourself to refocus.
- **Repeat daily:** Refocus.
- **Create the habit.** You'll sense an improved ability to listen, and will come upon new, richer and otherwise overlooked insights.

2. Get past fear to remove a listening impediment

- Fear is the enemy of discovery. What does fear feel like? Paralyzing? Hard to focus, think, listen? The goal of this exercise is to experiment with how you can reframe fear, and convert the associated energy into a motivating personal challenge.
- Get past fear by asking yourself, and then answering, two questions:
  - "What can I control?"
  - "What can I influence?"

You probably cannot control capital availability, but you can influence investors with a sharp pitch that demonstrates your passion and thoughtful customer insight, increasing your odds of getting resources.

Customer journey mapping template

Customer journey maps are most useful completed in conjunction with the user/buyer/payer/influencer assessment.

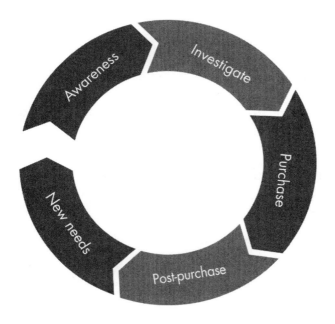

➤ Make development of the map a collaborative team activity.

➤ The goal is to create a separate map for each potential customer segment. It is early, so choices now are not set in stone and are "best guess."

➤ Choose one segment to start.

➤ From your insights, what do you know about each phase? What are the dynamics of users, buyers, payers, and influencers? Note: the customer may not be one person. They are more likely an agglomeration of user and buyer, affected by payer and influencers.

➤ What is each person thinking, feeling, and doing at each phase?

➤ Not sure? Then seek those insights as you continue discovery.

➤ Look for implications that will be useful to prototypes and business model assumptions.

➤ Create a map for each segment.

➤ Treat these maps as iterative and dynamic. Keep them available—even on a wall—as catchalls for further insights and implications.

Connections

Connecting to insights: Ready-to-use discussion guide

The setup: Whether you work with an expert or pursue insight gathering on your own, have a discussion guide ready in advance. Guidelines:

➤ Customize your own guide that addresses your concept and market;

➤ Err on the side of open-ended questions and probes;

➤ Avoid leading questions that risk insinuating the answer;

➤ Remember that tone of voice, not just words, conveys bias;

➤ Keep in mind that it's better to record conversations (with permission, of course) than risk the distractions of note-taking. Low-cost transcription services are available for digital files.

The questions—and not trying to prove you are right:

1. Tell me about yourself. (Name, where live, work, age, family, et cetera.)

2. Tell me about a typical day in your life. (For B2B, tell me about how things went yesterday at work, what is on your calendar this week, et al.)

3. Probe for insights:
   - "And then what?"
   - "And what happened next?"
   - "How did you react?"
   - "How did that feel?"
   - "What did you say?"
   - "What did you do next?"
   - "Show me what you were doing?"
   - "Why did you do it that way?"

4. What are the biggest frustrations you have throughout the day? Probe for times of day, and each example that comes up.
- "What did you do?"
- "How did you handle that?"
- "What did the other person do or say?"

5. Move to more specifics when your instinct is that you are in fertile territory.

6. Another productive path starts with, "When was the last time you (fill in relevant activity)?" Continue by uncovering each step and the reason behind it, who else participated, how it felt, why each choice was made, what other options were considered. Keep in mind that an answer such as, "I never do that" or "I haven't done that in years" is by itself an insight. There may not be much of a problem to solve, or the use case is so infrequent or inconsequential as to not represent the opportunity you imagined.

7. Try asking questions that introduce a relevant use case. For example, go back to the earlier ketchup story. If you were gathering insights, you may have had a hunch that the bottle was problematic, and asked something like, "Show me how you make a sandwich with condiments?" "How do you store condiments?" "Why do you do it like that?" or "Tell me how you do it?" You may want to be in a setting that allows for a demonstration.

Culture

Cultural attributes for successful discovery include:

➤ **Seeks** the new and unfamiliar, not merely confirmation of the known

➤ **Values exploration** of the unexpected and unfamiliar

➤ **Empathetic** towards people's emotional needs and values

➤ **Listens** more than speaks, and asks questions

➤ **Sensitive** to their own biases, and works to overcome them

Chapter summary

➤ Discovery is the starting point to find problems worth solving, and that align with your passion and purpose. Discovery comes from direct engagement with users, buyers, payers, and influencers.

➤ Listening—with all available senses—is the basic method to uncover signals and cues about emotional and rational needs. The best discoverers are active listeners who make a conscious effort to hear, observe, and understand people. They start with an open mind, and work hard to set aside biases.

➤ Active listening skills are essential and can always improve. Start by asking for feedback. Stop constructing in your head what you plan to say next while others are speaking, and you will already be improving.

➤ Behavior is the source of some of the best signals and cues. What people do, not what they say they do, is where the truth lies.

➤ The user/buyer/payer/influencer model applies to B2C, B2B2C, and B2B use cases. Together with customer journey mapping, the model helps surface actionable insights about motivations and behavior. What you learn applies to proto-typing, segmentation, positioning, business modeling, and even go-to-market plans.

➤ Insights challenge assumptions as they reveal unexpected patterns of customer behavior and non-obvious preferences or needs. Within a grown-up company, especially one depend-ent upon a pre-digital business model, a crisis may be needed to mobilize the organization to listen and act upon the impli-cations of fresh insights.

➤ Do-it-yourself discovery is workable, but carries the risk of confirmation bias. The change maker should be hands-on in discovery, not waiting for someone else to generate a report. When feasible, engaging a facilitator who has no stake in the solution itself can increase objectivity.

➤ Your relationships are a source of discovery participants and providers. With a general enough concept, techniques such as "person on the street" intercepts are also a great way to get started.

➤ Creating the V1.0 story based upon discovery findings creates momentum to gauge investor interest (whether that means the CEO or division head, or private investors for a startup opportunity).

CHAPTER 2:
Purpose, Passion, Promise, and Positioning

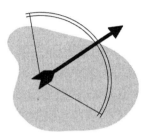

What is purpose and why does it matter? You've got insight; at least one problem you see people struggling with, and you are ready to create the solution. Time to get moving.

Having purpose is not a matter of writing a vision statement that ends up an empty slogan.

Purpose means knowing what you stand for—why you want to exist. With purpose backed by commitment, you can challenge yourself—and others—to put in their best efforts.

Purpose comes to life through:

➤ **Passion**—the commitment and strength of belief that fuels delivering on what you stand for;

➤ **Promise**—the expectations you set for the people you choose to serve;

➤ **Positioning**—how you portray and promote the promise.

Purpose defines the mark you want to make. Do you want to leave your purpose behind at the office doorstep? Or make your mark through the user problems you choose to solve, merging your personal sense of purpose with career and commercial pursuits?

Purpose comes from self-awareness, not brainstorming sessions or focus groups. It provides a basis for big and small choices. It triggers alignment across values, principles, and execution. When purpose is baked into the culture, things happen the right way and everyone knows what that right way is. And when there is a choice between the purpose-driven way and some other way, the team course-corrects. They work harder, work smarter, work better, have passion about what they are doing, and are closer to the brand's constituents. The purpose-driven way is more sustainable (and joyful), especially if more matters to you than delivering short-term numbers.

Purpose is the fuel that gets entrepreneurs and corporate innovators so fired up that they will not be deterred from turning insights into concepts, prototypes, business models, in-market experiences, and results. Purpose and passion breed the intensity for transformative results. They drive brand positioning from core beliefs and motivations into how to build your idea into a product or service.

Stories in this chapter demonstrate how purpose and passion shape choices, decisions, and actions to create the trajectory from discovery to results.

Change makers who put thought into defining their purpose and then connect it to execution energize others with their courage and commitment.

How can you figure out your purpose? Look within your life for signals:

➤ Read to expand awareness of your interests;

➤ Talk to others about their sense of purpose;

➤ Collect magazine pictures of images that attract you, looking for patterns that signal things you feel strongly about;

➤ Pursue your hobbies to further boundaries;

➤ Seize the opportunities arising out of personal moments of truth;

➤ Work on something that fits with your purpose, either in an already-built company, at a startup, or on your own.

Brand purpose inspired by personal experience

Stu Libby is Cofounder and CEO of ZipDrug, a New York City startup taking on the drugstore chains with an alternative patient experience. The two 800-pound gorillas, CVS and Walgreen's, together control between 50 and 75 percent of the market in fourteen of the top U.S. metropolitan areas.[1]

Stu spent over a decade as an ad tech executive, participating in the exit of DoubleClick to Google in 2008. Despite this accomplishment, for Stu, something was missing. "I knew my instinct to move on was correct when I told my new manager not to worry, that I didn't plan to be around for long, and he had absolutely no reaction," says Stu.[2]

Stu's dad became ill and, following a hospitalization, required prescription medications. The experience of transitioning from hospital to home, and getting prescriptions filled, refilled, and in hand was not merely messy and inconvenient, it could have been life-threatening. Stu saw an opportunity to solve a problem that not only had financial potential, but that also reflected his values.

Sure, a major goal for Stu is to generate financial returns, and he certainly knows what that takes. His goal is also to close holes in the business-as-usual journey from illness to good health. Stu is using technology, data, and partnerships to enable the corner-drugstore experience in the digital world—an experience that ZipDrug aspires to make proactive, relevant, compassionate, and connected.

As a seed investor, I get to hear many founders' stories. They often share how market needs are identified through personal experiences. In the best cases, personal experiences are followed by exploration of whether other people have the same or different needs, and in turn challenges founders to focus on questions of how their purpose connects to market opportunities. Why are they going after this problem? What is it they really want to achieve?

Can you pass the "walk over hot coals" test?

I like to understand founder motivations. Business cases and budgets, exit plans, and minimally viable prototypes are basic. Any entrepreneur also has to pass the "walk over hot coals" test: Do they demonstrate such commitment to what they are doing that they demonstrate capacity to walk over hot coals for, say, at least five to seven years, maybe more? Will they stick to it, or will their passion be diminished by daily pressure and frustration?

Think it's different in the corporate world? Think again. If you've ever had to decide whether to grant business-building resources to a team inside an established business, or have been on the team seeking funding, recall to what extent evidence of the ability to pull it off was a factor. Purpose and passion provide execution power in any company to master the daily challenges of bringing innovation to market.

Purpose and passion drive straight down into the details—the nitty-gritty of navigating regulation and other non-negotiable implementation tradeoffs and market conditions. Sticking to your intention minimizes dilution by the sum of decisions that gradually undercut goals. In healthcare, Stu says, "Financial success is in the bowels of the industry." At ZipDrug, from the CEO down, culture, policies, processes, staffing, strategy, and in-market activities are defined by the singular purpose which motivated Stu to found the company.

Purpose enabling value and growth:

➤ Is present in head, heart, and delivery;

➤ Has roots in market needs;

➤ Sets an organization's cultural parameters;

➤ Creates focus for execution;

➤ Motivates and energizes teams.

Make a virtue out of laziness

Reconsider the innovation premise if you assume you can change people's behavior. The most powerful default is the familiar. Prove that the innovation resembles something familiar to users, *and* that it is simultaneously the undoing of that familiar solution. Then, it is possible to get people to abandon what they know.

A mentor and globally recognized innovation thought leader once said to me, "Make a virtue out of laziness." This is not to judge anyone's work ethic—it's just another way of acknowledging that inertia is the biggest barrier we all have to trying something new. Make it easy for people to change, starting with making them feel they are not really changing—that they are doing what they already do, only better.

Create auto-magical solutions.

From purpose and passion to promise and positioning

With knowledge and commitment to your purpose, get ready to shape positioning, the tool to express purpose in words, images, and actions. Everything you do should manifest your positioning.

Positioning was not always thought of so broadly. Pre-digitally, positioning was a communications technique in the domain of the marketing team and the advertising agency. Today, ads and marketing communications are only the surface layer of how positioning comes to life for any brand.

Paul Barnett, a serial creator, and founder and CEO of Now What, The Creative Question Company, began his professional path in advertising, and is a trusted partner to leading brand executives. The common denominator among his clients: all are change makers. Paul is an innovation instigator. He is an active listener, insight-gatherer, interpreter, and question-asker. Paul has a special ability to translate what he sees into stories that inspire action.

What Paul is hearing and observing among brand executives is a movement away from messaging exercises built only on market research, and toward positioning executed as experience grounded in purpose.

In the pre-digital era it was okay to execute on a linear path. Hand the insights gathered through discovery over to functional experts working alongside marketing, sales, and product. Document requirements to prototype and build. Send these to engineering. Write the creative brief and review with the agency, who then creates storyboards and media plans. Meet with customer service to anticipate use cases. Work with legal to establish necessary disclosures. Finish the forecasts, and cut and paste financials into the plan. Develop selling sheets, and head off to the marketplace.

Now, Paul sees brand executives tying positioning to purpose, strategy, and culture. Time invested in brainstorming and conducting competitor message audits is being reallocated to discerning the nuances of value and growth creation. Macro trends are forcing change makers to challenge what used to be taken for granted: What business are we in? How do we infuse our positioning into our culture? "It's been surprising to me," Paul says, "how client attention to these questions versus the traditional notions of bringing product to market has itself become a trend."[3]

Paul's philosophy resembles Stu's ZipDrug strategy with what may seem like unexpected consistency, considering his clients are big, established companies, not startups. A difference: Startup founders get to establish their purpose from day one. They don't live with the overhang of a larger company, whose purpose may be unclear, at odds, or nonexistent. Setting or resetting purpose in an organization with a legacy takes leadership from the very top, and commitment to alignment down to daily operating details.

In the past, positioning efforts mainly influenced communications. Now, ads are like a transparent coat of gloss, and much more is required to execute positioning that is credible and compelling. Customers and employees may not be asking straight out for purpose, but more and more are affected by its presence and relevance.

So, what is the "much more" that change makers are taking on to get beyond marketing messaging? How are they getting to the substance of their brands' purpose?

They are asking questions and listening.

"If I were given one hour to save the planet, I would spend 59 minutes defining the problem and one minute resolving it," Albert Einstein said.[4]

Change makers are asking questions of customers, employees, and themselves to get to the truths of a business's purpose, and to confirm the links between purpose, business model, and executional and performance outcomes.

The 90s way and today's way

Lori Marcus chairs direct-to-patient engagement for Harvard Business School's Kraft Precision Medicine Accelerator. An adviser and board director, Lori has also created value and growth as a marketing executive at brands including Pepsi, The Children's Place, Keurig Green Mountain, and fitness startup Peloton. All of this experience has convinced her of why purpose must connect to culture and in-market execution.

Lori says, "There is the 'nineties way' of figuring out brand promise and positioning, and there is what must happen today."[5] Back then, positioning focused on finding the competitor hole that defined the point of difference, building a "brand pyramid," and moving from a wide base of features to the point of the pyramid—the point of emotional connection. Positioning execution focused on advertising and communications, packaging, shelf space, and sales support.

Today's way: Purpose is the foundation of a pyramid leading to positioning.

Positioning is a big decision, not to be shortchanged. To get it right:

➤ **Invest in the best expertise.** Apply good methodology. An external expert who can bring an outside-in view can add valuable insight and method.

➤ **Test out possible approaches by prototyping.** Try different ways to convey purpose and positioning to your key audiences to see how each works in content, in signature experiences, and in new features.

➤ **Lead an inclusive process.** Include different members from across the organization to get buy-in and create rich results.

➤ **Don't cut corners.** There may not be a quick ROI on the investment to get these both right, but the business model consequences will be enormous.

➤ **Implement proven rules of brand development and go beyond.** Bring purpose to life in go-to-market tactics spanning all customer interactions, not just marketing communications.

➤ **Give employees permission.** Give employees the authority and a stake to deliver the brand promise within and beyond marketing.

➤ **Recruit believers.** Bring in talent who believe in your purpose and want to contribute. Avoid nonbelievers who will be corrosive, irrespective of expertise.

➤ **Don't build without purpose.** What happens to a building that lacks a foundation?

Purpose and positioning-based execution take work. Applying principles that have been traditionally centered in marketing across functions requires a strong leap, especially inside companies used to vertical silos and within-silo cultures. But it's a leap worth taking because the result is a differentiated experience, and a stakeholder-focused way of operating.

So why do businesses, even when they do a great job on brand and offer positioning, fail to deliver experiences that are consistent with purpose? Execution requires aligning attitudes and behaviors—the many small pieces that make a culture—across the organization and business model. And the leader who aspires to change culture assumes the risk of breaking some glass. Capabilities must be adapted, metrics updated, silos flattened, talent exited and recruited.

Lori offers a point of view on a possible, albeit provocative fix: She imagines the CMO can be the "CEO of marketing," not the executive overseeing communications, research, and media. The difference? What if one executive has authority for the levers to attract and engage customers? Their mindset must be to orchestrate and lead, not to control. To deliver on the positioning 100 percent of the time, and not just as a communications exercise, but on every aspect of the business model that is a candidate for alignment.

Or, as Lori says, "If you are in charge of the brand, by definition you are helping to define the company," including culture. The chief customer officer or chief experience officer role comes in and out of fashion. The title is empty if the alignment across the organization is not enabled by CEO sponsorship, appropriately defined authority, shared purpose, linkage to brand, and a customer-centered, collaborative culture.

For an organization that historically hasn't done so, assimilating purpose can turn out to be too transformational. Employees will be excited about purpose that elevates their roles. They will want to get on board. But only C-suite leadership can drive the requisite culture shift. If the higher-ups aren't ready to change, the business cannot become purpose driven, and positioning will not show up beyond ads, sales, and marketing messaging.

If the status quo is not likely to change, the change maker committed to purpose may have to decamp to better ground.

Finding purpose as an outgrowth of insight, aimed early on at execution, is transformative—and worth the effort—for organizations accustomed to a more traditional product development paradigm who are now seeking to innovate.

Identify supporters, fence sitters, and resistors

Establish expectations up front of how you see:

➤ The process of discovery, and why it matters;

➤ The connection between purpose, business-model drivers, and results for which employees are being held accountable;

➤ The path to creating value and growth, including the ambiguity, iteration, messiness, and the amazing feeling of success;

➤ Managing the downside, including why no one will be thrown under the bus.

Walk in your team members' shoes to imagine their take on what's in it for them.

Have the conversations to figure out who is on board, who is undecided and open, and who is firmly entrenched in the past or some other direction. Bring the supporters into your fold, and work to win swing voters. The resistors? Don't let them wear you down.

Don't overthink the answers, which may be hiding in plain sight and just require that you pay attention, look in the right places, and listen.

Oftentimes long-tenured employees have a unique appreciation for the brand—including during what may have been brighter days—and carry the sense of purpose in their heads and hearts. You just have to ask them and honor their perspectives.

And of course, listen to and watch your customers. Vast data sources and sophisticated analytics tools are bringing new ways to understand the market. But simple, qualitative insight techniques should not be discounted, and can turn out to be invaluable. When Lori set forth to lead the positioning work as CMO at The Children's Place, she was delighted to hear moms recount amazing childhood stories about the brand. To a person, they talked about "play" and their wonderful memories of when the stores had playground-like structures—including a slide. Over and over, people's faces lit up as they talked about color and play. So for Marcus, the choice to lean into the optimism of childhood and the emotive effect of bright colors was obvious.

Implementing purpose

Leaders who understand and influence the culture's capacity to support innovation stand a chance at succeeding. Culture nurtures or destroys progress, affecting how everyone engages as missionaries to bring the purpose to life. Change makers run a gauntlet—encountering roadblocks, frustrations, and mistakes. That is the nature of their work.

Advice on how to build purpose into daily operations and culture:

➤ **Pick the right people.** Vendors, partners and contractors, and employees who are on board or can get there.

➤ **Use metrics and incentives that support purpose.** Stating a purpose and then acting inconsistently is self-defeating. Choose metrics that reward and recognize delivery.

➤ **Refresh the customer experience.** Align customer servicing, terms and conditions, and other communications and policies to an on-purpose experience.

➤ **Design processes.** Use data to design processes that facilitate versus obstruct. Help risk managers see themselves as change partners, not status quo defenders.

➤ **Communicate.** Invest time to communicate so everyone understands how to translate purpose into execution.

You have control over finding and achieving purpose. Not asking questions to challenge how well you are doing is not a change-maker option.

THE THREE Cs OF PURPOSE, PASSION, PROMISE, AND POSITIONING

Capabilities

The tools of discovery do not get put away once core insights are gathered. Use them for purpose and positioning, whether looking within yourself for personal insights, or among those who surround and affect the brand and its impact. Continuing to ask questions is a more important role than trying to know all the answers.

How to ask the right questions

1. **Say nothing.** Silence creates space for more insights. Some people find silence uncomfortable; they keep talking to fill the

emptiness. Others are grateful for the opportunity to reflect and organize their thoughts.

2. Ask for more. "That is so interesting, can you tell me more about that?" What's great about this question is it is an open-ended invitation, and avoids confirmation bias. Revelations won't come out until a few rounds of repetition.

3. Poke at claims for truth, but do so gently. "Wow, that's amazing—how do you know that?" is another great question-tool for a world where big claims abound, and are sometimes hard to connect to facts. Use this one to detect fabrications and overstatements, and to direct conversation toward tangible evidence.

Emulate Albert Einstein

At Now What, asking questions is the norm. Try the team's practice—a one-hour meeting each week, adhering to the "Einstein Rule":

➤ First 55 minutes. Everyone just asks questions. No answers allowed.

➤ The last five minutes. Come up with solutions.

➤ Avoid the distractions of note-taking.

➤ Watch for nonverbal communications, not just those that are verbal.

Employee orientation: The gift of three questions

New Now What employees receive "the gift of three questions" in a simple and memorable ceremony to bring each person into the company's question-asking culture. "It costs nothing and does more for your brand," says Paul, than typical new employee orientations. "It puts into action what we believe in and what we value."

Asking questions takes courage. Too many people fear that asking signals ignorance. Questions stimulating dialog will pull people toward the purpose and find their roles to deliver the brand's promises.

Connections

How to connect beyond the usual suspects: Creating a community of hand-raisers

Identify the change makers, influencers, and sponsors within the organization or your external network. Simply share what you are doing and your philosophy, and then keep track of those who respond with offers of help or advice, or other efforts demonstrating they are on board. Within a company this can take the form of department or division updates, or intranet postings. Within your network consider a quarterly personal newsletter. The community of believers made up of those who respond will be an expanding resource. You may be surprised by who steps up to assist.

Identifying the "hand raisers" is a high-impact, low effort technique, especially when resources are tight, that can seed rewarding relationships and opportunities. In one of my two stints as a chief innovation officer there was almost no staffing support. But I was able to uncover sleeper cells of innovators around the organization through internal communications. As a result, I built a list of people I could count on to bring expertise and elbow grease to projects.

A great one-liner to connect past to future

A certain amount of resistance to innovation happens when people tied to past success see the next big thing as a repudiation of their contributions.

You can take the edge off this emotional reaction by following a simple rule that will signal respect and empathy: "Compliment with an *i*, and then complement with an *e*."

Here's an example applied to the case of introducing client segmentation to a group of insurance agents among whom the norm for prospecting has always been to mine their own social circle:

"You have done an amazing job within your network figuring out who can benefit from our products. We can offer a new tool to try out that might allow you to build even better results by tagging your contacts with a segment identifier. Others are finding this is helping prioritize leads ..."

Culture

Cultural attributes for successful purpose, passion, promise, and positioning include:

➤ **Self-awareness**, showing a 360-degree view into their own strengths, weaknesses, passions, and principles

➤ **Conviction** to persist in the pursuit of their passion with the right amount of stubbornness

➤ **Critical thinking**, connecting dots and detecting patterns well beyond the obvious

➤ **Honesty**, above all setting the standard for integrity

➤ **Principled**, taking accountability for their actions, and never blindly following the rules.

Chapter summary

➤ Purpose defines what you stand for and why your business exists.

➤ You cannot build a business headed toward greatness without a purpose that inspires passion in you and everyone upon whom you will depend.

➤ Having purpose means going after solving a problem—one that is big and that you believe can be solved. Purpose-driven people are true to their beliefs, and inspire that standard in others.

➤ Purpose sets the stage to frame positioning, culture, and execution.

➤ What you stand for should show up in every aspect of product and experience, enabled by the actions that happen across the organization every day. Be sensitive to how things are happening, not just what is being delivered. Even what customers never see affects how they feel about your brand and offering.

➤ Messaging is just one element of positioning.

➤ The potential of positioning is realized when it frames policies, processes, how employees engage, the environment, skills, measurements, and what is recognized and rewarded.

➤ Asking questions carries far more weight than knowing the answers. Ask questions and be fully open to any answer. "Tell me more" and "how did you figure that out" are great constructive ways to build dialog and get insight.

➤ Change is hard when people aren't ready for it. Most are not volunteering. The greater the perception that past success is somehow no longer good enough, the more big change can feel like a negative. So, be sure to "compliment, then complement": Honor the past and bridge between that familiar past and future vision.

CHAPTER 3:

The Art of Being Resourceful

Finding, shaping, and implementing innovation takes resources. The obvious ones are people, money, technology, equipment, and materials. You may be on a team where you see a better way to do things, or are being asked to go after white space. Perhaps you join an organization where being the new guy allows you to see things with a fresh eye. Or you are striking out on your own, and personal bandwidth, bank account, relationships, energy, and skills only go so far.

Whatever the starting point, change makers end up changing *how* the product is created, not just *what* the product is versus whatever came before. And the stronger the status quo, the more likely the need is for basic resources to overcome obstacles. Maybe you are working with immature, unproven technology, or regulatory approvals take extra effort because the rules didn't foresee what you want to do. Daily encounters with processes, policies, and mindsets feel wearying.

You can counter the drain on money, time, and talent by being resourceful. Resourcefulness is:

> ➤ A high payoff must-have for any change maker in any context;

➤ A force multiplier on every penny, every hour, line of code, every ounce of materials invested;

➤ A virtual stockpile of options to turn to when obstacles hit.

This chapter delves into what it means to be resourceful. Stories from some truly resourceful change makers bring to life what this special bundle of skills and traits looks like in action, and what it means in environments from the earliest stage to highly developed businesses.

Are you an execution superhero?

Recall the last time you tried to do something that hadn't been done before. Or think about how an admired entrepreneur took the first steps to advance their idea far enough along to make believers of friends, family, and others, providing initial capital to get off the ground.

Some founders have rich uncles. But most investors—be they your divisional CFO, friends and family, or venture capitalists—have to be convinced that your concept is a great use of capital and time. In fact, not just great, but the best alternative versus whatever else they might choose to do. These days, funders are well aware of the near certainty that more resources will be required than that first pitch ever imagined. They know that they will invest time, not just dollars.

Resourcefulness separates the funded from the unfunded. Can you avoid derailment by finding quick and clever ways to overcome difficulties? Do you get energized at the thought of having to come up with how to get through the craziest impediments to progress?

The unfunded idea person may say, "I have a terrific idea, but I cannot get the money."

Funding is abundant for resourceful teams with insight-driven concepts who have a plan and show they can deliver in spite of the unplanned. No, that is not a crazy statement. In the corporate and startup worlds, when capital providers say, "We simply don't have the funds," dig deeper for the real reason. Perhaps the real message is that you are talking to the wrong investors, or that you are working in the wrong company or culture, or that you have not proven that you are a superhero of execution. A no may also mean you have hit a wall that only your own resourcefulness will knock down.

Change makers are dogged enough to get the first vote of confidence that initial funding represents, then execute the plan, sticking to dates and budgets. They find the path forward no matter what. They work the ins and outs, the unexpected, the good news, bad news, great news, and terrible news, knowing the news before it even happens. They live steps ahead in the future. Living in the present means being too late and burning resources in a game of constant catch-up.

Plato had the right idea:
"Necessity is the mother of invention"[1]

Meet Drew Lakatos, CEO and cofounder of ActiveProtective, a health tech startup whose invention is best described as an airbag that deploys automatically from a belt to reduce injuries and deaths occurring when seniors fall. His purpose is to solve a tough problem that can save lives and preserve quality of life.

Senior falls in the United States are creating medical and social crises, at an estimated annual economic impact of over $30 billion. According to the Centers for Disease Control, in 2015 close to three million seniors landed in U.S. emergency rooms because of falling. These are just the identified falls; millions of falls are suspected of not being reported.[2] Falls are also the most common cause of traumatic brain injury.

In 2005, Drew and his wife, Kelley (a physician's assistant

specializing in trauma care), attended the holiday party at St Mary Medical Center outside Philadelphia, Pennsylvania.

Among the attendees was Dr. Robert Buckman, director of the Trauma Unit. Their serendipitous meeting that evening turned out to be seminal for ActiveProtective.

Suddenly during the celebrations, pagers went off, indicating an airlift to the Emergency Room of a Level 4 patient—the second-highest urgency level. Drew said, "I was invited to go to the Trauma Unit to watch the process. I had never seen a trauma procedure or my wife in her realm. I wanted to understand what really happened."[3]

The patient was an eighty-year-old woman who had been having Christmas dinner at home with her family. She lost her footing on a flight of stairs and went down. She suffered a serious head injury and broke her pelvis and both legs.

Drew said, "I sat there, thinking about the inefficiency of us just waiting. All of a sudden a helicopter landed and the team erupted into action. This woman was lying on a stretcher. You could tell from how she was dressed she was a person of means, and there she lay, fighting for her life.

"Not long after, I saw my wife heading to the family waiting area, obviously to inform the family that they had lost a beloved family member. It was all over in fifteen minutes. She died from the injuries she had suffered because of the fall."

Drew saw the woman's death as an avoidable tragedy caused by something we all do every day without even thinking—going up and down stairs. Background research showed the magnitude of the problem. Dr. Buckman shared all he had researched, and the two knew they had to take action. "I wanted to do something for the planet and for humanity," he said.

Obvious question: Why wasn't this problem already solved? Well, others had sort of solved it. Existing solutions ranged from thick, protective padding inserted into tight-fitting spandex undershorts, alarms and sensors to notify an attendant of a fall after the fact, even helmets. These products were aimed at nursing homes and senior living residences. Garments were restrictive, and hard to put on. They reduced quality of life. They were a reminder of lost mobility and independence. Not surprisingly, these products saw limited adoption. The need for a better answer was there.

Dr. Buckman shared with Drew his inflatable cushioning concept designed to pop open instantaneously. The design would be thin enough when collapsed to not be uncomfortable, and as easy to put on as a belt. It would offer life-saving performance, but without discomfort.

There were just a few challenges.

First, the technology was at least a few years behind the vision, so the price point at which the device could be produced would be way too high for meaningful adoption. There were two technologies essential to delivering on the protection promise: a sensor kit to know within a split second that it was time to inflate, and a cold gas inflator (something like a CO_2 container). This all meant a waiting game for the technology to advance to the performance standard with reasonable economics.

Drew's resourcefulness enabled him to master the waiting game.

Second, realize that Drew created and stuck to a strategy for continuing to support his family, be a continuous learner, and pursue his purpose. In the early days of the company, he was a father of three, with a fourth child on the way. In his heart Drew is an entrepreneur *and* a husband and dad. His strategy? To do what he calls "duty cycles." Work in corporate for a few years, learn a new technology, jump out, and start a company. If there's a payday, he moves on to the next startup. If not, he goes back to a corporate paycheck.

Other steps:

> ➤ Drew gave much thought to what type of investors to bring in—people who wanted to get high returns *and* who had shared passion for ActiveProtective's purpose.

> ➤ He assumed six months to get funded, but to plan conservatively he gave himself twelve. In the end it took sixteen.

> ➤ He focused on recruiting people who wanted to solve the enormous challenge of a cost-effective, high-performing, comfortable way to reduce the incidence of severe injury and death resulting from senior falls.

As a result, he overcame the chicken-and-egg dilemma that traps many ideas on the napkin back. Drew said, "There are a million great ideas. The interesting thing about the evolution of our idea was that research suggested it would work, but until initial investors came in and funded device development far enough along to produce legitimate evidence, we couldn't move forward."

The most remarkable moment in Drew's story was how he went about assembling the device prototype that would allow testing to generate sufficient evidence that the product would deploy quickly enough and at the right moment. "People were asking, 'how do you know it will work?' We knew we could tune the air bag to deploy correctly, but everyone was asking, 'how can you be sure?'

"One day I grabbed my son and ran to a junkyard in search of non-bloody air bags from wrecked cars. I took the inner tubes out of my bicycle tires so I could make a sort of bladder inside the air bags to adjust the loads. I got an invitation to do testing at a VA mobility lab. I showed up with a suitcase full of airbags that I had cut out of junked cars, with bicycle inner tubes installed inside, sewn together by my dry cleaning lady for two bucks apiece. We were able to beat the best product on the market. We had the data we needed to prove effectiveness."

The resourceful leader profile

Resourceful leadership depends on mindset. Technical capabilities help, but matter less than being able to see and plan for potential derailment before it happens, and having a get-it-done attitude. The resourceful change maker refuses to give up, but they are not stubborn to a destructive extreme. They are undaunted by the conflicts inherent in changing the status quo; in fact, they are energized by the potential contribution they can make.

Resourceful leaders have a positive outlook and as a result tune into solutions. This means they are:

➤ **Optimistic.** Believe that there are ways to face down hard and non-obvious problems that others may miss.

➤ **Re-framers.** Possess an auto-activated ability to see old issues, situations, even data in new ways that lead to answers and options.

➤ **Attentive.** Their explorer wiring is tuned in to picking up insights about big, unsolved problems.

➤ **Curious.** Want to learn more. Drew tuned in to the senior falls problem at a holiday party, and because he chose to observe the trauma unit in action.

➤ **Creative.** Inventive about working with whatever is on hand to develop prototypes, even where others may see just junk.

Resourceful leaders treat others with respect and value people as people, and as a result, inspire and attract others to enable their purpose. This means they are:

➤ **Self-aware.** Know their own strengths and limitations, and are humble enough to seek help from those who support and complement them.

➤ **Collaborative.** Recognize that by inspiring others to bring what they can to drive the business's purpose, their capacity to execute expands.

➤ **Engaging.** Emit a magnetism that draws others in.

Resourceful leaders can execute under diverse circumstances, especially through adversity. This means they are:

➤ **Pragmatic.** Pursue big problems and solutions with a down-to-earth, get-to-work attitude, getting past the limitations of existing solutions.

➤ **Focused.** Aim skills, resources, and energy to achieving purpose while not diluting effort on low payoff activities and decisions.

➤ **Impatient.** Move forward with urgency to create and live in the future.

➤ **Hands-on.** Do not sit back and wait for others to dirty their hands. Their instinct is to learn and make progress by doing.

➤ **Energetic.** Create self-propelling sources of energy to work through complexity.

➤ **Prepared.** Do the homework to understand all dimensions of challenges. They are good at figuring out when to dig into the right details.

➤ **Anticipatory.** Pursue a personal life management strategy that frees them to pursue their purpose. Whether it's extreme discipline or moving back in with family to cut expenses, the resourceful leader creates the foundation for clear-headed and dedicated focus.

Talent attracts talent

Drew's approach applies in any change maker situation, in any context—for a startup founder or the corporate innovator seeking to get a concept off the ground.

Inside an already-built company, there are plenty of obstacles even at early validation points. A big challenge can be gaining access to what any new concept needs most at the beginning—discovery insights, or hands-on support to generate proof points. Maybe this means engaging a developer to write some code, or an analyst to dissect data, or a designer to do a mock-up, or a scientist or lawyer to lend expertise. Locating and engaging the right people can be more difficult than finding capital. But without this support, new ideas run out of steam before ever getting that first bit of funding.

Certain people like to take on big challenges. There are always those who want to be part of achieving a larger purpose. These are the "army of the willing," and they are out there eager to connect. Inside a big company, surfacing the right people can happen with as simple a tactic as the right communications on the intranet, sponsoring an input session (free food always helps!), or just walking the floor. Recognize and reward those who pitch in. They will keep giving, and bring along more like-minded contributors.

A global CEO once said to me, "Talent attracts talent."

Resourcefulness takes creativity, not just penny pinching

Resourcefulness has an element of watching how much money is being spent and on what. But being resourceful is not about restricting use of color printer ink, telling the team to take the cheapest flights, or engaging in nickel-and-dime directives that make any team groan. Such requests can be perceived as petty, and inflict damage on morale above whatever money is saved. If a culture is built on resourceful behaviors, this stuff is implicit and never has to be a voiceover. Better to put effort into the bigger message: how to shape a culture where everyone on their own wants to find ways to achieve the purpose. Then everyone is driven to make the best use of dollars, time, and talent.

Change makers don't wait for resources to be allocated or approved. They tinker and find a way. They have a knack for tracking down the best resources and taking advantage of the vast capabilities that are out there. They search and use the many free or low-cost tools widely available in our self-service world.

Being resourceful isn't budget-dependent. Quite the opposite—resourcefulness liberates you from always seeing budget approval on the critical path. As the saying goes, constraints breed creativity, whether those constraints are self-imposed or brought upon you. Drew Lakatos lived this as he combed junkyards for airbags from totaled cars that could be reused to prove the viability of a sophisticated medical device.

Resourcefulness means accountability from beginning to end

David Cooperstein is a veteran digital executive who has worked in telecom, retail, and media. With typical humility, he is a self-described "marketing and strategy guy." On either side of establishing the first CMO offering for Forrester Research, he has held executive roles at pre-startup to mid-stage venture-backed firms, as well as mid-cap public companies. David has that rare combination of strategic insight and foresight, turbocharged by a pragmatist's view of how to get from ideas to actions to outcomes.

David's philosophy about resourcefulness is typical of his cut-to-the-chase-style, and echoes and expands upon Drew Lakatos's story. For David, resourcefulness demands being able to combine opposing traits as a:

➤ Doer, not just an orchestrator or facilitator;

➤ Curious executor, not just an intellectually curious thinker;

➤ Simultaneous tactician and strategist;

➤ Multitasking juggler of right- and left-brain-driven skills;

➤ Futurist, grounded in the present.

David distinguishes between what it means to be a manager versus a change maker. He says, "The manager lives in a chain of command and sees his role as getting directions from across and above, driving the directions down, and overseeing the team. He gets told what to do and gets others to do it. The resourceful change maker takes on any executional task at a moment's notice, and does whatever is required in the context of the bigger picture. He sees his role as to do and help others do, not to oversee and observe."[4]

The resourceful change maker approaches tactics strategically. An example: A marketer may be tenacious and effective implementing next week's lead-generating program. But if that program, and the next one, and the one the week beyond those first two, drive lead volume but conflict with brand purpose and positioning, that marketer ends up dissipating resources. They are squandering the brand and confusing potential customers. Conversely, delivering each lead program on-brand creates cumulative, perennial rewards, not just short-term results.

Multitasking juggling means taking on many issues, tasks, deliverables, challenges, and strategic issues all at once. This does not mean being an expert at everything. Knowing what you do not know, accumulating new skills, and knowing where to turn all take on greater importance when it is simply not possible to be the expert all the time.

Finally, resourcefulness requires being a futurist with the mindset of an owner. Think about a startup, with few customers and little or no revenue. To be ready to serve customers and demonstrate revenue potential, the team builds ahead of demand. The pressure is on to have an accurate crystal ball outlook, along with deep accountability to see the best tradeoffs despite a fuzzy view of what might happen.

In David's world, resourcefulness means doing more with less, and getting further faster by:

➤ Knowing when to say no;

➤ Setting expectations about what will be done by when;

➤ Communicating the right message, in the right channel, at the right time;

➤ Not aspiring to perfection—knowing when good enough is good enough;

➤ Accepting unpredictability as the normal state of affairs;

➤ Proactively pitching in to get stuff done;

➤ Asking for help;

➤ Taking accountability for outcomes;

➤ Being able to sit back for five minutes and determine the fit with the strategy, decide yes or no, then move ahead.

Being resourceful is about knowing how to improvise

Improvisational theater is a place where all of the elements of resourcefulness come to life. Trained improvisation artists are models of resourcefulness.

Marian Rich is founder and president of Career Play, Inc. She is a New York–based improvisational theater performer who helps people use her stage techniques in other domains, including innovators in classrooms and companies.

Improvisation is learning by doing and creating on the fly. "Improvisation lets you as the participant be who you are becoming, rather than be as you are," Marian says.[5] "We all have the capacity to be other than who we are, and we all grow and develop during our lives." What is a change maker doing as they move their vision to reality if not becoming something more than what they are today?

The basics of improvisational theater can be learned and practiced by anyone. No technical skill is required. Marian's approach and that of her fellow performers is based on the empirical research of Lev Vygotsky. Vygotsky, a Soviet psychologist who also studied linguistics, was fascinated by the connection between language and child development.[6] His theories apply through adulthood, played out on stage and in the settings of everyday life.

Are you a "yes, and" or a "no, but" person?

The core principle of improvisation is captured in two words: "Yes, and." If you can use the phrase "yes, and" to promote dialog, you are capable of improvising. In fact, if this is your habit, you are already improvising. And if you are good at improvising, you will be a more resourceful change maker.

Why do these two words have disproportionately high impact? "Yes, and" is an active listening behavior. Chapter 1 discussed the role of active listening to figure out people's needs, including those not expressed verbally. During discovery, active listening expands and shapes possibilities. In the case of resourcefulness, active listening expands and shapes access to more and better expertise, technology, capital, equipment, workspace, and other requirements for progress.

"Yes, and" behavior invites creativity and constructive problem-solving. It signals that ideas are welcome, and eliminates the public criticism that kills new, fragile concepts. It acknowledges that connected idea fragments form the eventual answer.

In the world of improvisational theater, "yes, and" is the performer's hand-off to the next step in the story's creation. Like a performance troupe, team members working at a white board designing an experience or solving a tough coding challenge can be "yes, and" participants.

By doing so, each team member expands the group's capacity within itself to do more.

Maybe you've been in situations where people assume that creativity is a distraction from the task at hand. The truth is, the creative capacity of a group where members listen and acknowledge diverse thoughts is superior to one where a dominant group member saps everyone's energy trying to prove they are the smartest person there. The change maker, by allowing everyone to contribute and honoring everyone's input, eliminates the constraint of only being able to access what is immediately available, obvious or known.

A 2012 global survey by Adobe found that three-quarters of people surveyed indicated they do not believe they are living up to their creative potential.[7] Have you witnessed the nervous reactions of colleagues when they are asked to contribute creativity to a challenge? Marian says, "People don't appreciate each other's or their own creativity. Everyone comes with a lot to give. If the environment is strong—if people are saying yes, and listening to each other with openness and desire to accept what others are offering—if they add to them and build with them—everyone's creativity will be unleashed."

"No, but" behavior is degenerative. It shuts down the ability to build upon peer contributions to problem solving.

Unfortunately, "no, but" is a default behavior in pressured situations where shutting down dialog with a view to time efficiency actually has the opposite effect: to de-energize and deplete resources.

Having doubts? With a small group, try this two-part exercise:

Form two teams. Ask each team to take five minutes to plan a party with an unlimited budget. There are just a few rules: Each group must create the party as a team, and is allowed to say, "no, but."

See what happens. How effective is the team?

Now repeat the exercise, and in this instance everyone must say, "yes, and," and cannot say "no, but" following others' contributions.

Now see what happens.

Who among us has not complained about how the lack of a budget makes achieving a goal tougher? The truth is, even with unlimited budget, the creation of something new rests more upon the dynamic created by two words, two syllables, six letters, than by money.

Lessons from improvisation expert Marian Rich:

➤ Cooperating and completing each other vs. competing with each other is resourceful behavior;

➤ By virtue of practicing the simple behavior of "yes, and," anyone can create an environment where resourcefulness is a habit.

THE THREE Cs OF RESOURCEFULNESS

Capabilities

A DIY model to reframe

Reframing is a technique that allows you to see problems or gain insight that would otherwise be missed, by making it possible to see things from a different angle. Anyone can get the gist of how to reframe, and practice to improve. In fact, you already may reframe, without even realizing.

Reframing requires setting aside current beliefs. Because it is a way to get beyond the constraints of a singular point-of-view, reframing is a close cousin of "yes, and" behavior. Like "yes, and," reframing offers a way to avoid getting trapped by a too-narrow perspective.

Think about a camera. When the lens is in one position, you see a scene a certain way. Moving the lens in and out can change how you see the exact same scene. Reframing empowers you to push your inner lens to a better position.

While it's not as easy as letting the words "yes, and" roll off your tongue, the A-B-C-D model is a useful way to create a reframing habit.

In sequence, ask and then answer four questions:

➤ What is your assumption?

➤ What are your beliefs stemming from the assumption?

➤ Challenge your beliefs.

➤ How can you now look at things differently?

Create a four-column table and pick a few assumptions about the innovation you are pursuing. Any assumptions come with constraints, even if they are not at first obvious.

LIMITING ASSUMPTION	BELIEF BEHIND IT	CHALLENGE THE BELIEF	DIFFERENT APPROACH

Let's try an example that is easy to understand.

➤ Assumption: people pay for daily purchases with credit cards, and will continue to use these devices to pay;

➤ Belief: a card is the accepted way to access one's line of credit for daily needs;

➤ Challenge: cards are not necessary; a line can be accessed through other means;

➤ Different approach: embed the line of credit in mobile devices.

Assessing the resourcefulness of people you may want to work with

How can you tell if someone is resourceful if they are not someone you know? Follow these conversation guidelines to ferret out a few concrete examples, and use the listening questions from prior chapters to learn more.

The key question to raise is: "Tell me about a time when you demonstrated [fill in the resourceful behavior] to accomplish a goal or take on a tough challenge."

➤ Surface stories of what really happened.

➤ Steer away from speculation about what the right action "would be."

➤ Convey that you want to hear about real situations, not concepts or philosophy.

➤ Give permission to say "I," not "we." (We are trained not to do this, but now "I" answers are constructive.)

➤ Ask follow-on questions, such as, "What exactly made you come to that decision?"

➤ If you feel you must ask, "what would you do?" questions, apply a high discount factor to the answers.

Connections

What does networking have to do with resourcefulness? If you buy into the theory that what matters is not what you know, but knowing who to ask, you will quickly see that a broad and deep network of relationships to which you contribute is itself a huge asset.

Thought starters to build and sustain your network

➤ Put yourself in situations where you can meet new people. Reach beyond people who seem to be just like you.

➤ Accept invitations to speak at and attend events. Being a panelist offers an opportunity to get onto the stage with limited advance prep.

➤ Commit to attending one or two monthly events—social, professional, or related to a personal passion.

➤ Ask people you admire what events they attend and get on distribution for announcements and invitations.

➤ Remember, meeting great people can be as serendipitous as it may be planned, so allow for serendipity.

➤ Set a goal for how many people you will meet one-to-one each month to exchange perspectives on topics of mutual interest and value.

➤ Do not wait to reach out to people until you need something from them. Your reputation will tarnish. Reach out to people when you can help them.

➤ Go for volume. According to the theory of the "strength of weak ties," people with greater volume of weaker ties get closer to resources and opportunities.

Create a practical approach to keep track of your network

➤ Establish your own CRM (contact relationship management) process;

➤ Don't get hung up on the software tool—what works is what you find easy to use, not what has the most bells and whistles;

➤ Use a system that you will stick to for adding new contacts, updating information on existing contacts, and establishing and implementing descriptive tags.

Position yourself for quality social media connections

The right personal profile and content-sharing and blogging strategy will attract followers or invitations from people with shared interests.

➤ Do you come across to people you would like to know as someone they also would like to know?

➤ Is your bio current, professional, specific, and authentic?

➤ Do you generate or share useful content that signals who you are, and that is of interest to your network?

➤ Do you express a point of view worth hearing?

➤ Do you communicate your purpose so people can feel it?

Caring for your relationship network can make the difference when bringing your ideas to market, and achieving their potential for impact. So there is more to come on strengthening your network throughout the *Playbook*.

A further tip for outreach to your network

Keep your network current on what you are up to by sharing insights helpful to them. Experiment to find the right rhythm and frequency.

Genuine relationships are based on giving, without strings attached. When these sorts of relationships exist, people will be there for you in unexpected, unpredictable ways.

Culture

Cultural attributes for resourcefulness include:

➤ **Transparent,** open, honest, and accountable

➤ **Urgent,** recognizing that speed is a currency

➤ **Constructive,** showing "how to" instead of "why not"

➤ **Hard-working,** heads-down and hands-on to make progress

➤ **Collaborative,** working together to solve problems, meeting a higher standard than cooperation

➤ **Full of intellectual *and* executional curiosity** to figure things out by doing

Chapter summary

➤ Resourcefulness is the force multiplier for getting more out of resources, so you make progress even when capital, time, and talent seem limited.

➤ The first ingredient for resourcefulness is passion about purpose.

➤ Resourcefulness is reflected in behavior. Seek to surround yourself with people who are role models and contributors to your own resourcefulness.

➤ The resourceful leader is simultaneously a strategist and deep-in-the-weeds doer. Their approach to short-term objectives makes whatever is coming next faster and easier to accomplish. They do not create rework and do not mortgage the future for the present.

➤ Resourcefulness is demanded from the one-person startup to the big grown-up company.

➤ Be a "yes, and" person, and discourage "no, but" behavior to compound the creative potential of the team, find nonobvious solutions, and shape a productive culture.

➤ Since resourcefulness is demonstrated in behavior, change makers can use proven assessment techniques to screen for these behaviors.

➤ A good network is a capability for greater resourcefulness.

PART II
SEEDING

"When I have fully decided that a result is worth getting
I go ahead of it and make trial after trial until it comes."[1]
Thomas A. Edison, inventor and businessman

When I went back recently for my first visit since childhood to Thomas Edison's West Orange, New Jersey, lab, I saw evidence everyplace of why Edison is viewed as one of the greatest inventors of all time. The 1,093 United States patents bearing his name are central to his legacy. What further struck me as I wandered through the facility was his dedication to prototyping, and how it was Edison's way to discover ideas and translate them into commercial products.

Remarkably, Edison kept on hand thousands of samples of just about every kind of material imaginable. He continuously enlarged his collection, which he saw as a source of inspiration and enablement. He focused on turning new ideas that might lead to functioning, feasible models into prototypes that could eventually be manufactured, distributed, and sold at scale.

Edison role-modeled the behavior and mindset that drive ideas to prototypes and then to commercialization. Beyond working in the lab, he was committed to figuring out whether business models supported his inventions. He addressed operational and manufacturing requirements, and never abandoned testing and learning to uncover new breakthroughs and confirm fit with the market.

Section I presented the basics of a change maker's wiring:

➤ Intellectual curiosity to power exploration;

➤ Passion and clarity about purpose;

➤ Resourcefulness about always finding a way to make progress.

Section II tackles the skills, tools, mindset, and capabilities that get concepts to take hold. *Seeding* means change makers will test market conditions to see if they are right, and be willing to adapt. They will experiment, commit to trial and error, face down ambiguity, and surround themselves with people who amplify their vision and purpose. They will work on getting a mix of many elements right, so that their concept stands to meet its potential to become a business that:

➤ Is economically sustainable;

➤ Solves real problems and reflects empathy for users;

➤ Executes on the change maker's vision in a world of surprises and unknowns.

Change makers move quickly and iteratively to validate their concepts. Can it be built? What are the right skills, perspectives, materials, equipment, technology, and talent? Do people want to buy? Who are these people? Does the concept work for users? And who are they? What is the best way to get the product or service into their hands? How do they value it, so what should it cost? How do the answers to these questions lead to a business model? Will the financial outcomes be convincing to investors and provide a good return on effort?

Chapter 4 shows how to make progress. The short answer has three pieces:

1. Create increasingly precise prototypes,

2. Put them into the hands of users, and

3. Be savvy about harvesting and applying new insights.

To begin, accept that perfection is not the goal. The right standard of performance—whatever is "good enough"—is the place to begin.

Prototyping generates clues to shape the business model—the focus of Chapter 5.

A business model must convince investors. But the dollars don't come your way because of polished financials. They don't depend upon the inevitable year-three growth hockey stick. In fact, conveying excessive certainty early on will backfire. Savvy investors will see inexperience and naivete in overly precise financials that cannot possibly be calculated early in the game.

More important is to figure out how to get stuff done—quickly, intelligently, pragmatically. Well-conceived execution plans increase the odds of forecasting and achieving reasonable financials. Strong financials are the outcome of sensible execution plans that capture the "must do's" and "how's." They have nothing to do with clever manipulation of a spreadsheet.

Building a business that tweaks an existing offering is relatively straightforward. The change maker's challenge is to figure out what might happen when a concept is unprecedented. How much evidence do you need? How do you convince yourself and then convince investors? How do you make up for the lack of a rearview mirror's worth of data?

Guaranteed, whatever goes to market will lack perfect insight. There will always be room to improve and adapt. On top of persistent ambiguity, there will be complications and unexpected problems. The change maker will be better equipped to stare down surprises with planning and project management that account for a nonlinear and unpredictable world.

Chapter 6 addresses how to deliver in a world where there is no such thing as a crystal ball. The alternative? Sharpen your ability to see problems before they happen, be ready with contingencies, and capture unexpected opportunity. Getting these instincts and behaviors right comes from understanding yourself and building the support system to complement and expand the strengths and assets that got you where you are.

Farmers who plan to seed a field with a new crop, or plant in a new field, go about their work differently than if they are replanting last year's crop in last year's field. You are introducing a new seed, perhaps to a new market. You are engaged as an explorer, you have established your purpose, and are reaping the benefits of resourcefulness. You are ready to apply the tools and recommendations of Section II so your concept can take hold.

Prototype, Test, Learn, Iterate

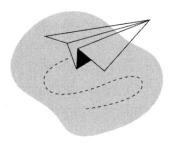

Apple, Inc. cofounder Steve Jobs is credited with discrediting the value of market research.[1]

After all, since people cannot describe what they need, or do so only relative to what already exists, what is the point of asking? Leave it to the product people and designers to tell users what they need.

Maybe that is not exactly what Jobs meant.

For sure, traditional approaches to market research have limited value to uncover the insights that fuel disruption. That is why the concept statements and storyboards of the past are being replaced, or at least complemented, with iterative prototyping processes that engage users. Prototyping opens the door for users to co-develop concepts. A good prototyping process focuses on:

➤ Creating models,

➤ Letting users engage with them,

➤ Learning from the interactions, and

➤ Creating versions that are progressively closer to being market ready.

A good process may look and feel informal but is disciplined and based on principles.

Most people have an easier time reacting versus creating from scratch. Not surprising, since we live in a world where the volume and complexity of choices make reacting a practical necessity. So expecting others to envision how you can help them, with no stimuli beyond questions, is less constructive than giving them something to which they can react.

Interpreting Jobs's take on market research as justification to build products without user input misses the point. Change makers already know they can get clues about needs by examining the workarounds people create to solve problems on their own. Users may not be able to verbalize needs, and are less likely to imagine innovations that step far away from known experience. But behaviors and emotions transmit signals. Engaging users in prototyping puts you in a position to intercept these signals and witness direct feedback.

Engaging users in iterative prototyping means embracing new ways to validate product and service constructs.

A major newspaper publisher wanted to stop a readership slide. The circulation team felt the problem was that content did not address readers' interests. They conducted interviews to find out what people wanted to read. The feedback was "more local sports." So a weekly section on local sports was added.

The management of that newspaper probably added an ounce of weight, and cut down thousands more trees. And guess what? They didn't get one new subscription. That's because people don't really change behavior based upon how well their interests are satisfied.

Matt Foley, introduced in Chapter 1, says, "It's the job of the users to tell you their problems. It's your job to create solutions."

Prototyping defined: Tinkering meets purpose

The origins of prototyping are rooted in everyday activities of daily life that we all experienced during childhood.

Prototyping is a way to learn. Engaging users in a live rendition of a product or service, however rough, narrows gaps between a great idea inside your head and a tangible, functional and sought-after real world product.

For anyone innovating in the sciences, technology, or manufacturing sectors, prototyping describes the first and subsequent pre-production expressions of a product or experience that guide the specifics of usability and feasibility. Building prototypes and letting users play with them begins to uncover answers to questions like:

➤ Does it function?

➤ Does it do what it was intended to do?

➤ Does it hit quality standards and expectations?

➤ Can it be replicated at scale and at what cost?

➤ Does it solve the problem it was intended to solve, and does it do so effectively?

➤ How does it perform relative to existing alternatives?

➤ What reactions does it evoke for potential users?

The process works for a deceptively simple product like a spoon, a complex medical device like a dialysis machine, or a digital experience powered by algorithms and big data. Prototypes allow the abstract to become concrete and the imagined to become real. As models are exposed and repeatedly modified, concepts move closer to market readiness.

Prototyping is in play in everyday processes that advance learning. Think about tinkering, a habit that has existed throughout history. Thomas Edison, our hero inventor, was arguably one of the great tinkerers of all time.

Seen through the lens of child's play, prototyping is just a way to figure things out. Contrary to being a domain of technically trained experts, life experience proves that even a child can do it. So, barriers to prototyping are low. Because it is such a familiar, intuitive practice, creating and sharing prototypes also offer a way to build user, team, and investor buy-in.

Art Chang, founder and CEO of Tipping Point Partners, sees it like this: "A prototype is the minimum product that enables the creator to generate real feedback from real users. It's the basis for ongoing iteration."[2] Such iteration moves a concept one step at a time toward launch.

THE WHEN, WHY, HOW, AND WHO OF A PROTOTYPING PROCESS

The When

When to begin to prototype is a judgment call. In principle, prototyping best begins as soon as you can put something tangible down on paper, in code, using materials on hand. Capture the intention as soon as you start to see elements of your idea. Artistic skill is nice, but certainly not required.

Ben Zombek is an industrial designer and entrepreneur whose career began with companies including GE and Kodak in his hometown of Rochester, New York. He shifted toward startups, in order to experience greater innovation diversity. In 2010 he launched BZ Design, a product, user interface, and marketing firm that helps clients shape what he describes as "the total package"—design, hardware, user experience, and marketing.

Ben believes in engaging early when the widest range of innovative possibilities is open for consideration. He prefers to initiate prototypes while underlying technology is being defined, before there is even a commercial application. He says, "There is a lot of amazing technology that isn't fleshed out yet into a product. We like to work on building the 'believable packages' at the earliest possible stage when scientist and designer can join forces."[3] Once patents are issued, commercial product restraints emerge.

Ben engages with universities, and develops working relationships with scientists in campus labs, enabling his goal of early involvement.

The BZ team starts by sketching as many ideas as possible on paper. Soon, designers also work with foam, to brainstorm in three-dimensional space. Their principles:

➤ No idea is a bad idea.

➤ Simpler is better.

➤ Feature overload craters prototypes.

Ben says, "The goal is just to get something out on a piece of paper. We use a very fast and loose process. We go for volume. We'll start to see that some attributes of one sketch work well with those of another. The sharpies are moving fast as the team fills more and more sheets.

We pin things up on boards, all around the work area. Then afterward, maybe the next day, we reconvene and evaluate. No one shoots down ideas. We naturally work to see the merit in each sketch, each foam model."

By working together, team members inspire each other, and end up creating "our" ideas, not piles of separate ideas where each thought, each sketch belongs to an individual.

Aliza Freud founded SheSpeaks in 2007 to elevate and amplify women's voices. With 250,000 network members—and monthly social media reach of over 300,000,000—SheSpeaks is a powerful tool for brands to connect with women for insights, user-generated content, and to magnify their messages.

Among SheSpeaks' innovations: creating a virtual and limitless alternative to generate consumer insight, debunking the orthodoxy that study participants must be paid, and demonstrating the power of users-as-content creators to partner with brands.

Speed is survival in the social media space, so Aliza and her team never stop iterating the SheSpeaks experience. The goal: to go live with each new version of the platform as soon as possible, to view the latest prototype and the in-market experience as one and the same. The company develops enhancements, pushes them out to see what works, then changes or scraps on the fly.[4]

Not every business has this flexibility. But any change maker should aim to iterate toward a minimum viable product ("MVP") that meets two criteria:

1. Solves for the original problem statement

2. Motivates users' interest strongly enough to get them engaged

No matter the business or sector, "early" and "fast" must be the rules of thumb for prototyping. Art says, "When and how to begin is subjective but always situation-specific, based on a defined use case grounded in real-world needs."

The Why

There is nothing like seeing and interacting with the real thing to:

➤ **Identify functional requirements.** Translating vision into concrete form forces execution details to be acknowledged. What will product dimensions be? What materials will be used? What will the user experience navigation be like? Can partners deliver on promises? Does the prototype meet or defeat hypotheses about whatever user assumptions have been made until this point?

Trial and error is the only way to figure out how to make new concepts work. Drew Lakatos's story in Chapter 3 shows how even junkyard materials can become mock-ups of what in final form will be a highly sophisticated medical device.

➤ **Spot and avoid easily missed mistakes.** Ben's team worked on a wearable device for asthmatic children. Ben says, "What looked fine in an initial prototype turned out to be way too large when we had an eight-year-old in front of us. We immediately realized that the engineers had to shrink the electronics components." The team avoided a near-certain failure point. Component sizes were reduced, thousands of smaller wearable devices were sold, and production ramped up.

➤ **Understand user emotion.** Emotions shape perceived value and utility—drivers of commercial potential—that otherwise would be hard to predict at this stage. How a physical product feels in a user's hands, what interaction is like, how intuitive the product is to use and whether size, shape, and weight are right for different use cases are best determined by engaging users. These interactions produce data on how people use products, and reveal via body language, verbal intonation, and facial expression how products make users feel. The same holds for digital products where product dimensions lie in navigation elements, messaging and imagery.

➤ **Foster collaboration.** Prototyping nurtures creativity, and motivates rallying around a concept to make it real. Teams that embrace prototyping stimulate innovation—testing and learning, engaging with users and with each other, and experimenting without fear of failure. These behaviors become essential for raising money, too. Whether investors are corporate executives, angels or venture capitalists, "show and tell" builds understanding between founders and funders.

➤ **Move faster.** While adding multiple steps of iteration to test and refine feels like a slowdown, prototyping speeds up getting to market with an offer that works and that people want. Think of the difference between a fully unfurled piece of string and a string of the same length, compressed into a coil. Prototyping is like the coil—more gets done in a lot less time.

The How, Part One:
Inspiration, Purpose, and Strategy

Sameer Vakil and Summi Ghambir are cofounders of GlobalLinker, a Mumbai-based startup born at a New York City Starbucks.

These cofounders are motivated by a need they have witnessed over years living, traveling, studying, and working across the United States, Asia, India, and Japan. Their insight: small and medium enterprises (SMEs) are the backbone of the global economy. Around the world, SMEs create more jobs, grow faster, and demonstrate greater capacity to innovate than larger enterprises. Yet they face disadvantages largely due to lack of economies of scale and limited access to funds. Larger companies have these advantages, and take them for granted, while SMEs spend a lot of time and effort to address needs that are not core to their businesses.

"SMEs are beloved as a totality, but at a unit level, as a practical matter, they are neglected," says Summi.[5]

The two asked a simple question that led to a massive vision: Why shouldn't a small business have big company advantages? What holds them back, irrespective of sector or geography? Small and medium businesses would all like to grow.

Or, as Sameer likes to say, "While we refer to them as small and medium enterprises, their dreams are never small or medium."

GlobalLinker has set its sights on how to make the big dreams of small business owners attainable. The experience integrates the essentials to run a business—the to-do's that should not distract from generating sales, developing products, and building relationships. GlobalLinker makes it easy and fast to:

➤ Find people, services, capital and deals,

➤ Plan travel,

➤ Design and launch a website or ecommerce store, and

➤ Access a host of services, products, and benefits on pre-negotiated terms.

"Small business owners never stop working, from the time they wake up until the time they go to sleep. Whatever their device, you will see about nine windows open as they chase multiple demands. They work so hard. Yet they have told us that when they leave for the day, the most important tasks they started the day wanting to do end up neglected," Summi says.

Sameer and Summi credit their progress to immersion in the small business owner persona and problems. Their move from the back of a napkin to global platform has happened by:

➤ Identifying and exploring a big and deep unsolved problem for a large, growing market segment;

➤ Defining their purpose and positioning;

➤ Executing and advancing successive prototypes shared in labs, closed pilots, and then small-scale live trials;

➤ Having commitment to execute.

The How, Part Two:
Step-by-Step Prototyping

The GlobalLinker team prototyped methodically. Their step-by-step path:

> ➤ **Segmenting the market.** Three clusters were defined: service, product, and service plus product. For each, hypothetical solutions, starting with words on paper, were developed.

> ➤ **Text-only prototyping.** By spending time in workplaces, they saw the problems firsthand and used their observations to create these first prototypes. Three priorities were set: business networking, efficiency tools, and access to economies of scale.

> ➤ **Low-fidelity prototyping.** Also produced on paper, based upon conversations with users about what their days were like.

Summi says, "We let users mark up paper models to show what changes would make the experience better. Then we asked for details. We focused on finding the most meaningful use cases." Next steps in the process:

> ➤ **Thin prototyping.** This meant developing an on-screen experience with no backend—a clickable prototype to validate how users expected to interact, and what words and phrases users found most meaningful. This phase made it possible to get rid of jargon and internal speak, and use relevant, common sense language.

➤ **Getting to the alpha phase.** Because the GlobalLinker developers were so methodical in gathering and applying user feedback through each prototype, there was little rewiring to do. Now, one hundred users had access to a live site with a functioning back end.

➤ **24-month in-market beta.** Unlike the alpha, which included business owners considered to be "friendlies," the beta included self-selected users who came across GlobalLinker and chose to participate. The beta goal was to be sure that everything functioned smoothly and that users saw utility.

➤ **Redesign.** The team combined beta feedback and the prior several years of effort, undertaking a significant redesign.

➤ **Results.** Big usage and engagement upticks occurred, including performance gains 300 percent above predictions for a key partner. The hard work also translated into cobrand partner contracts. As of this writing, GlobalLinker is preparing to expand across nine markets and is already live in three countries.

The best advice about prototyping from Summi and Sameer:

➤ **Begin with a clear and well-articulated vision.** "We have always been passionate about building the best small business community. Our vision: To make the growth of small and medium enterprises simpler, more profitable, and enjoyable," Summi says. The team focuses on what matters most to users.

➤ **Decide up front what kind of organization and culture you want.** Summi and Sameer see team and culture as their secret sauce. Sameer says, "In 2009, we spent forty-five minutes at that Manhattan Starbucks writing our plan, and we are still sticking to it. We spent three full days deciding what kind of organization and culture we wanted, and how we would create both. We truly believed that culture and co-ownership would allow us to multiply our own dreams, not just ensure productivity."

➤ **Dream big and stay the course.** Have conviction about what you seek to do, but flexibility about how you do it. Avoid the temptations of the short term, or you will short-circuit your plans.

➤ **Recognize what prototyping is really about.** First: the technique—the skills of building the iterative models toward product-readiness. Second, the purpose you set for your business that got you to be a change maker. Clarity of purpose aimed at a big market need is most of what defines prototyping.

The GlobalLinker cofounders believe that their success has resulted from vision and purpose first, method and mechanics second. "The difference between innovation and adaptation is this: If you want to adapt, it's more about technique. But if you are innovating to disrupt or transform, don't go anyplace without first knowing your purpose," says Summi.

The Who: Users

Never take users for granted, or underestimate their input.

Users may not be sitting at the worktable or standing at the white board with sticky notes in hand, so it is every team member's job to keep users' perspectives present.

"Users," Ben Zombek at BZ says, "are overwhelmingly interested in co-developing." They will give generous feedback if they see you are at the early stages. But if you bring them in too late, and a prototype seems too finished, users will be more likely to go along with whatever you present.

That is why the GlobalLinker team opened up user participation a bit more for each new prototype, moving from limited non-public, to limited and non-publicized, to limited public access to their experience.

At SheSpeaks, there is barely a distinction between testing and launching. New code can always be released, and the upside of leaning forward outweighs the risk of error.

The commonality between the two companies is that the teams decide how, when, and to what extent user engagement with prototypes should occur.

The Team

Resources are always tight and there is no formula to assemble the right prototyping team. The sector and the concept itself are factors. Individuals with wide skills may be able to wear multiple hats. What about user experience, marketing, sales, legal, data security, compliance? Concepts must ultimately meet non-negotiable standards, and also meet user expectations for privacy protection.

Follow this principle. "Include all of the stakeholders whose buy-in is going to be necessary for approval of my prototype," Art Chang says. "It is just common sense that the timeline to production will be shorter if everyone is brought into the process at day zero." Be clear about who is most important to get to a valid MVP. "Valid" means proving feasibility and showing evidence that there is market demand.

Sometimes teams take a narrow view of whom to engage to build that first working model. There are natural biases at startups toward tech gurus. Founders live with resource constraints, so they must be tight-fisted about paying for more than is absolutely necessary. Big companies contend with a different risk: allowing too many cooks into the kitchen. The politics of achieving consensus drive team membership and roles. Well-intentioned people weigh in and water things down.

Either path can be fatal. The best case is to walk the fine line of insane focus and inclusiveness. Be a cheapskate, putting just the right people on board. Invite those who have core, constructive roles. Ensure anyone who joins is bought in to the purpose.

When technology was driven by waterfall development, teams operated more as rows of individuals working along an assembly line. The steps came one at a time: document requirements, identify features and functions, create paper-based prototypes for user tests, and hand off to a designer to create a highly polished piece of work, then hand back to developers to build to the design specs.

This linear process is being abandoned as product managers and designers become collaborators. Designers are evolving into positions of greater influence and impact. They are moving away from creating designs implying surface finish, to delivering intuitive, sensible products and experiences.

"The more influence the design people have, the better," says Ben Zombek of BZ. "You cannot just put people in a cubicle farm and say, ok, time to be creative. Team interaction is crucial. You cannot say they are important to success, and not give them power or authority."

To traditionalists used to waterfall development, modern proto-typing's all-hands-on-deck approach may look risky. But, the truth is, any diverse and collaborative team that quickly and iteratively builds and tests improved prototypes has a better shot at success. Why? When the people who create are also those who maintain and operate what goes to market, accountability is built in.

Thoughts on capabilities

Prototyping decisions are driven by data and qualitative insight. Any web-connected offering is a source of data about how users navigate. Look for indicators of likes and dislikes, what they understand and what causes confusion, what is most important versus unnecessary. Combine behavioral data with qualitative feedback about users' needs and how they confront problems in daily life.

Determining what capabilities are best for prototype development depends on the context. Product prototypes demand different capabil-ities than those that are digital only. "Say you are dealing with a physical product," says Art Chang. "You will throw away each successive proto-type. There are limits to the number and role of testers because each has to have the product in hand."

But there is good news. Wider access to 3-D printing and declining costs are redefining product prototyping to become more like software development. This has tremendous implications. One of the biggest benefits is the declining limitations on user engagement in prototyping. The philosophy of software development has long been that the only legitimate feedback comes from users using the software in live envi-ronments. This philosophy is now edging into the physical products domain.

THE THREE Cs OF
PROTOTYPE, TEST, LEARN, AND ITERATE

Capabilities:

We're off to see the wizard ... to build early prototypes.

At the beginning of the change maker's pursuit, resources are especially tight. Feedback is essential, and depends upon a prototype. But building a prototype takes resources and requires feedback. There is a way out of this loop.

Having a shareable prototype doesn't require much if any code early on. The *Wizard of Oz* technique gets its name from the film classic, in which the wizard behind the curtain injects manual support to create a realistic, immersive experience for his visitors. The technique was named by Johns Hopkins University PhD student Jeff Kelley, who noted the analogy in work he was doing as he worked on his dissertation.[6]

Accordingly, the technique uses artifacts such as paper drawings, presented with a voiceover, or backed up by a video-supported user experience simulation. Together, these elements can create a sufficient sense of the user interface to get early direction—prior to putting effort into a more polished design. Look for free content online including specific examples of how to take advantage of this technique, which is faster, cheaper, and easier than putting effort too early on into the real thing.

Constraints breed creativity

➤ **Develop a prototype in under twenty-four hours.** Exaggerating a behavior can help reach a goal. So, give yourself just twenty-four hours to develop a prototype and see what you can create with a few collaborators who share your passion. You will be amazed at the progress that is possible. You will also challenge preconceived notions of how much time is required.

➤ **Contain scope of V1.0 to the top three features.** The Rule of Three, well practiced, never fails. Avoid feature creep. It's an unfortunate by-product of smart, creative, energized teams. A simple technique: make a list of the features you believe should be included. Then, circle the top three. A team can use a simple voting process whereby each person gets three votes. The features with the most votes make the cut for the MVP. Stick to it.

➤ **Abandon perfection.** Being a perfectionist will crush your ability to create the V1.0 prototype. Perfection seekers inhibit risk-taking that leads to innovation, and inculcate a fear of failure. The standard for measurement is how users see the ideal, not how you see it.

➤ **Don't wait for the exact right timing.** Timing is never right, and there is never enough time, enough money, the perfect mix or level of talent, or the best workspace. Rise above these self-imposed constraints and make the liberating leap that getting your prototype into the hands of users reduces obstacles.

➤ **Build momentum by iterating.** "Fail fast, fail cheap" is easy to preach, hard to do. Failure occurs when learning is not applied to the next prototype.

➤ **Use free and low-cost tools and resources.** Modern prototyping capabilities are within reach on a per-use basis. Online platforms are reducing the limitations of traditional research methods, and allowing sharing of visual prototypes or private URLs with invitation-only user groups. There are many options to support a live alpha or beta, especially for software-based products.

➤ **Take specialist skills off the critical path.** Use every resource, from your own network to crowdsourcing platforms, to close short-term talent gaps. Warning: be clear on what skills, self-sufficiency and judgment are needed, and don't compromise on talent quality. Be willing to admit that not finding the help you seek through your network may signal it's time to expand and strengthen relationships.

Connections:

The change maker cannot go it alone for too long. Creating and testing prototypes requires multiple skills, likely in advance of securing funding or establishing a formal team. So, a network of relationships to tap into may be the bridge to progress.

Within an existing organization, individuals who believe in the concept will go above and beyond whatever their job descriptions are. Seek these people out. Recruit a volunteer army to get started.

More on networking

1. Tips Learned Through Trial and Error:
   • **Don't make excuses.** Effective networking does not require you to be outgoing, extroverted or famous.

- **Ask for help.** We all have a need to be heard. When asked, others will help. Some won't, but most will. Reticent about admitting you have a problem? Just reframe the request from "I don't know what to do" to "I'd love to know what you think."
- **Much networking value happens serendipitously.** Networking value doesn't grow on a neat timeline. Investment over time in an always-expanding, cared-for network produces amazing, unforeseeable benefits.
- **Be authentic, and see networking as the chance for you to give.** If you are a giver, the best people in your network will give in spades. Remember, giving is in the eyes of the recipient. Giving means no strings attached.
- **Have fun.** Viewing networking as a burden makes it a burden.
- **Embrace it.** Networking is not a distraction from what you want to accomplish. It is a means to accomplishment. Feel you don't have time to network? Only meeting others immediately helpful to your goals? You are cutting off opportunities.

2. Eight Networking Boosters
   - **Set goals. What gets measured gets done.** Set a weekly goal of a number of networking interactions.
   - **Have a strategy.** Create a communications brief for yourself—define goals and tactics to build and enrich your network, including outbound and inbound tactics.
   - **Always bring value to the other person.** Too many people call upon others to ask for something they need, at the moment of need. Offer new insight, content, information, or a beneficial introduction.

- **Balance targeting and volume.** Don't overthink networking prospects. Sometimes the best people turn out to be those whose value is not obvious based on professional labels.

- **Stay in regular contact.** Don't expect anyone beyond your tightest inner circle to know what you are up to much less care, without you making an effort to keep them in the loop. Meet people in their environments, not yours. Match the cadence, tone, and type of any digital updates to meet your network's needs.

- **Listen.** Networking is about encouraging others to share with you, not to download to them. Imagine that for each conversation you have, your audience should do 70 to 80 percent of the talking.

- **Don't assume LinkedIn is the core platform for your network.** LinkedIn is fine as a source and is one of many sites where you might post your content. It's an entry point to bring people into your network, and to join others' networks. But remember your control over targeting, content distribution, and timing is limited, as is the opportunity to obtain metrics.

Culture:

Cultural attributes for successful prototyping include:

➤ **Always proactive,** never waiting until tomorrow

➤ **Passionate about purpose,** aspiring to serve users

➤ **Fast,** setting aggressive deadlines, and connecting speed to quality

➤ **Accountable** to deliver outcomes, not activity

➤ **Collaborative,** including actively listening, and team members with diverse backgrounds and skills

➤ **Open-minded**, exploring non-obvious thoughts raised by others

➤ **Objective about redirecting** by giving feedback without getting personal

➤ **Not perfection-seeking,** focused on getting to what is good enough for the current phase

➤ **Values and creates a motivating environment** full of creativity, curiosity, and urgency to succeed

➤ **Listening**, including actively encouraging others to contribute, acknowledging what they have to say, and accepting diverse communication styles.

Chapter summary

➤ Prototyping is a way to figure things out and learn by showing and engaging users with models of an offering. Building prototypes and engaging users for feedback is the best way to understand a concept's viability, usability, and desirability.

➤ We all tinkered as kids, so we all have some prototyping DNA. Prototyping is tinkering with a special pace and purpose, discipline, and principles.

➤ Prototyping leads to answers about the product itself, clues and insights that inform the business model, and evidence of viability and commercial opportunity. Prototyping creates momentum to win investor support.

➤ Prototyping starts with vision and purpose, and is fostered by a culture that enables and expects collaboration between product, design, other experts, and users.

➤ "The sooner the better" is a good rule of thumb for when to build and share the first prototype. Early and tangible is far and away a better goal at the start than finished and perfect. Users will be more candid reviewing a rough cut than one that is too polished.

➤ Artistic skill is not required. Pull out paper and pencil, and start to sketch.

➤ Common principles of prototyping apply across sectors, products, services, and experience offerings.

➤ The ideal team to create prototypes includes those who will be accountable to produce and operate the final product. Design talent is most effective when treated as a true partner.

➤ Resourcefulness is tested to produce great prototypes. All around you are your relationships, and free or low-cost tools to help get traction irrespective of your budget.

CHAPTER 5:
Business Model Linchpins

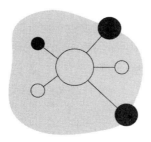

From a vacation beach chair in 1976, Citibank CEO John Reed penned a vision to transform the retail banking business model. His "Memo from the Beach" was a handwritten call to action to replace a deposits and loans business with one based on customer experience.[1] The memo, which went from words on paper to trigger the reinvention of retail banking, continues to circulate today among Citi alumni.[2]

Mastercard global board member Steve Freiberg joined Citi under Reed's leadership. Steve says about Reed, "Here was a guy who was young but senior. He went to his boss and said, 'I've got a great idea. I am going to take a machine and stuff $50,000 into it and leave it in the lobby of a bank branch. Over the weekend after we go home people can come and go, and take money out as they please.'"[3]

The guys in suits, starched white shirts, and pricey silk ties sitting on executive row must have thought Reed's vision was crazy. But he persisted, and moved Citi to disrupt the sleepy model of Monday through Friday, 9 A.M. to 3 P.M. branch banking. In so doing, Reed defined the business model parameters for what is now a given—a twenty-four/seven banking experience where people bank when, where, and how they prefer. Mobile devices, artificial intelligence, voice recognition, and other capabilities continue to expand what "anytime, any-place" means, advancing the vision seeded over forty years ago.

Reed's vision would not have become real without a viable business model. Nor would his then-daring aspirations have been possible without being able to execute massive transformation. Creating a new relationship between banks and their customers meant:

➤ Challenging the team to reframe the bank's purpose, from one based on pushing financial products to one based on understanding and meeting customer needs;

➤ Connecting what was not obvious yet technologically possible with what mattered to users;

➤ Breaking orthodoxies inside a large, complex organization;

➤ Seeing value in a totally new customer experience.

A complete front-to-back view

Imagine drawing a business model visual on a wall-sized panel, not as a financial model, but as an implementation path reflecting many levers and interconnected cranks. Some levers and cranks are controllable. Others only change as a result of impacts several times removed.

The nirvana state is to foresee and influence the movement of any lever or crank. Doing so depends upon having a complete front-to-back view of the business model—one that goes all the way from having a strategy for serving a market, to executing plans and achieving results.

The business model for twenty-four/seven banking came to life as the service experience in the ATM channel, the customer service platform, and in the brand tagline: "Citi Never Sleeps." Once twenty-four/seven banking went live, learning continued about customer segments, preferences and behavior, how each impacted revenues and expenses, and how best to deploy technology and data. The business model became a live, evolving ecosystem.

To set up the possibilities for your business model, start by answering these six questions:

1. How do you plan to make a significant difference for the people you intend to serve?

2. What is the size of the market? How many users and buyers are there?

3. How do sources of revenue connect to your point of difference?

4. How will you execute the strategy, manage the business-model levers, and maintain your point of difference?

5. What resources are required?

6. How do plans translate into financial statements, organization design, policies, processes, and infrastructure?

The business model design should capture how the business operates. A concept cannot become a business without a business model. Great ideas, even those that users love, are of no value by themselves. Being able to articulate the business model is a test of readiness, and exposes the holes that must be filled to move ahead.

What are the inputs to create the business model?

The business model synthesizes the work and thought invested to:

1. Gather insights from users and buyers

2. Assess trends and make assumptions about their future directions

3. Establish purpose and positioning

4. Muster resources

5. Prototype, listen, observe, adjust, and iterate

Perspective of a corporate CEO

Having benefited early in his career from John Reed's leadership, Steve Freiberg instigated and sponsored an innovation "skunk works" operation within Citi's credit cards business. His direction to the team: challenge norms, innovate the experience, aim to execute at scale. His exact direction when he asked me to lead the effort: "Make us more innovative."[3]

The skunk works team fostered ongoing dialog about game-changing business models spawned by customer insights and technology trends with a focus on:

➤ Foreseeing the trends that could rewrite industry norms, and that suggested big, emerging problems for segments the Bank wanted to serve;

➤ Prototyping to expose concepts to users;

➤ Developing Version 1.0 business models to stress test assumptions;

➤ Figuring out feasibility and scale requirements.

Many concepts never went beyond whiteboards. What mattered, even when concepts died, was the healthy debate each fueled. I was lucky enough to be a part of these efforts so I learned lessons about the impacts of culture, leadership, focus, and diversity on innovation in the field.

Getting to the business model: Culture and leadership

Leaders work through internal obstacles to change especially when a culture is so proud of its past that letting go is hard.

All fingers point to culture when things don't go well on corporate innovation teams. To paraphrase a common diagnosis, "Incredible idea, great research results and plans. But the culture ..."

Culture derails corporate innovation more often than lack of resources or skills. But the problem with pinning the blame on culture is that individuals get to sidestep accountability. That makes failure inevitable. Culture is called out as something separate, with a life of its own. But, a culture is the sum of decisions and choices, words and actions made by the people who belong to the organization, as well as those they choose to invite in. Culture is set by the top executive, and then carried out by how people choose to behave and treat others based on what they see at the top. The finger-pointing people *are* part of the culture.

Getting to a viable business model demands experimentation. If the team does not have the leadership backbone to create space for failures, that new model will not be found. Sponsorship is essential, but the daily dynamics of the culture are throughout the team, and help others persist against odds, show guts, and act with urgency.

Be the culture and lead others instead of debating culture and leadership. Stay centered on:

➤ Redefining the user experience by improving it in ways the market could not even have thought possible until you came along;

➤ Imagining how to attract customers, operate, and deliver value that upends the status quo—create a competitive gap;

➤ Executing at scale by delivering the experience with quality and predictability, at large volumes;

➤ Defining metrics that include market share *and* expectations for profitability;

➤ Keeping resources constrained, even in a corporate setting where money may be sloshing around. No more than a skunk works team is needed to find market needs and translate them into concepts—a team build-up can wait. In fact, having too many resources is detrimental.

Apply these principles and you will leave the competition flat-footed and bewildered.

Referring to the introduction of ATMs, Steve says, "No matter how smart you were as a competitor, you could not make the old process efficient enough to compete with twenty-four/seven banking." Three factors working together created a complete paradigm shift, and an experience that overtook traditional competition from the start:

1. Twenty-four/seven access to physical cash;

2. Twenty-four/seven customer service;

3. The "Citi Never Sleeps" message, which drove awareness and understanding leading to adoption.

The only limitations, overcome on a widespread basis in the mid-1980s, were interstate banking laws that had early on limited Citi's efforts in New York State.

People make a business model, not numbers

Can an established enterprise incubate and launch new business models?

Well, it depends.

The "yes" odds are higher when the organization invites in outsiders who are not wedded to traditions, who bring metaphors from other sectors, and who are able to connect the dots between old and new. Outsiders break through orthodoxies. Other conditions:

➤ **Sponsorship**. An engaged and visible leader with authority—the top executive—ensures outsiders and anyone else with alternative views are not repelled. Change makers colloquially refer to this as the "antibody" issue.

➤ **Culture**. A collaborative, listening environment exists, where people are curious to explore and try ideas that they haven't yet experienced, or can be created with the sponsor's leadership and determination.

➤ **Diversity**. A diverse team will get further faster, including outsiders who see possibilities sector or company insiders miss.

Take the example of the credit cards industry.

How were credit cards purchased in the pre-digital era? Up until the late 1970s, customers went to a branch, requested and completed a paper application, and waited six weeks for an approval or rejection to come by mail.

The change to direct, virtual customer acquisition at category behemoth Citi happened only when people were hired who knew nothing about the credit cards business or, for that matter, about banking. But they understood two things: multivariate scoring to drive underwriting, and how to envision a national versus state-based footprint.

These outsiders figured out that by using credit bureaus, people could be preapproved for credit. They envisioned and put a preapproved application into the mailbox, with the single requirement that the applicant sign their name. No surprise, iterations were required to get the process—and the financials—working. But within a few years, outbound direct-to-consumer marketing became the category's dominant source for new accounts. This innovation proved to be a stepping-stone to the digitization of the sector that picked up momentum in the 1990s.

A founder's perspective

Listen to Diane Hessan, chairman and founder of C Space, part of global agency Omnicom. Diane's litmus test to build a successful business model: "To dream about solving a very big problem in a unique way. You know you are doing that if people will pay for it."[4]

The business model takes market findings and assumptions a big step forward by translating prototype results, bets, and trend outlooks into what they mean to every aspect of implementation and financial assumptions.

In sharing the C Space story, Diane says, "When we started, we wanted to build something clients would love so much they would keep coming back. We wanted to help big brands get insights they never had before."

C Space became a respected provider of online communities to gather insights for global brands. The company is a case study in how to leap from prototype to business model, and from business model to big business. Stories within the C Space story show how the team set aside market research orthodoxies, and in the process defined a new product category.

Making a bet on trends

The team assumed the Internet would change the relationship between customers and brands—including how brands would learn about and from users. A "cut and paste" to digital channels of the existing models for market research would deliver faster, but not better.

Instead, C Space aimed to capitalize on trend predictions and potential client insights to create what had previously been an unimaginable level of value for clients.

Pricing and offer duration

Early on, the business model anticipated a fixed fee and a three-month minimum. C Space assumed that three months would be sufficient to demonstrate value and motivate contract extensions.

But during client pilots, the team realized that substantive value began at four months, and increased the longer the community ran. This led to three key offer and business model decisions:

1. The base offer was moved up to four months. As value grew, the offer was expanded to a one-year minimum with monthly billing.

2. This longer duration resulted in a c-suite dream come true: predictable financials. Two-thirds of the following year's revenue was projectable on December 31.

3. The offer and pricing strategy strengthened the business model. When clients saw value, C Space was rewarded with growth. This was not a business built on the downhill slope of slippage where sellers win short-term financial rewards when users stop using. It was a "we win/you win" model.

Defining and winning the target market

The C Space team wanted to work with big brands, and set out a sales and distribution strategy to open doors to decision makers.

"We knew that we would not sign big brands with a bunch of kids in a call center cold-calling for appointments. We stayed far away from that strategy. Instead we took a look at what kind of executives we would need to call upon, and hired a small, senior sales team with the presence and knowledge to engage with these prospects," says Diane.

Of course, this choice supported large-client revenue assumptions, and the associated expenses for account staffing, compensation, and sales force incentives.

Deciding the offering scope

One of the biggest decisions was whether to remain a technology platform or to wrap consulting services around the technology.

Two stakeholders saw two different answers.

Venture capital investors believed a services line would drive down margins and create unpredictable financials.

But clients had a different perspective. The company was selling the platform, but then leaving clients to figure out how to activate and leverage their communities. Clients were recruiting participants on their own, determining and administering incentive payments, and synthesizing hours and hours of community participant input.

This delivery model created at least two risks:

1. A more complicated decision to buy, and

2. The possibility that weak implementation by clients could lead to dissatisfaction and defection.

"Anyone can facilitate a community, but most people don't have the time to do it well," Diane says. "Clients were starting to tell us, 'do you know how much I would pay if you would do this for me?'"

The answer turned out to be a lot. Consulting services helped C Space grow faster by removing the barrier of having to figure out all of the implementation tasks. By stepping in to set up and manage the communities, C Space assured a quality experience. In the end, the company added services to its offering, doubling average revenues, and increasing client satisfaction in the process.

The C Space story is an example of how client experience and strategic and operational decisions inform the business model. Sorting through the options to get to answers forces a shift from big picture concepts to financial and execution consequences.

How investors assess business models

A short answer from an anonymous investor: "How do I know how a good business model? It is a little like pornography … I know it when I see it."

For the head of a new venture, accepting funding means becoming accountable to investors, whether the business unit head within a company, family and friends, seed investors, or venture capitalists buying your pitch.

Head in another direction if you believe you have an amazing concept and path to market, and potential investors evaluate your business model through the lens of the past. A rearview mirror can be useful, but is crippling when misapplied. Be clear about how investors interpret your business model's potential, and the criteria that play in to their decisions.

What do investors cite as the biggest business model downfalls?

➤ Not getting congruence between what you are selling, how long it will take buyers to begin to pay, and how much money is needed as a bridge.

➤ Failing to get customer feedback routinely.

➤ Hiring the wrong people.

➤ Raising money when money won't help.

➤ Not knowing when it is time to scale.

➤ Getting quickly enough to a sense of the value you are creating, including the pricing strategy.

The venture head will make or break the business

Bill Benedict, managing director for Alpine Meridian Ventures, says, "Whatever the business model may be, far and away the most important factor is the CEO's ability to roll it out and to change it."[5]

And that CEO must be heavily involved in the sales process. They are selling the product or service every day. They are hearing, "this is a really good product, but what I really need now is …" and they adapt to the customer's need.

Other investors support Bill's viewpoint. A strong business model depends on the core value to users, and as a result, the appeal to buyers. In businesses such as social networks, value is created for a user group who may be paying nothing (although arguably they are "paying" insofar as they are giving up data and privacy). The buyers are sponsors and advertisers. Their needs must be satisfied and their pain points also addressed.

Test and pivot, and don't put energy into elaborate presentations

Kauffman Fellow Jonathan Hakakian cofounded and co-leads Sound-Board Angel Fund with partner Richard Magid. He looks for how companies have evolved as he evaluates investment opportunities.

"Success," Jonathan says, "always comes with evolving. There are always changes that need to be made."[6] He looks no further than Sound-Board itself, which began as a consulting firm assisting entrepreneurs with their special needs, to then take on developing and managing the Fund along with an investor-driven screening and due diligence process.

Jonathan sees continued change from any founder's early concept as a positive. He says, "When I think about the companies in our portfolio that have been there the longest and are hitting success milestones, the entrepreneur's business today is strikingly different than what it was when they started with when we invested. This reflects their ability to react, be coached, and roll with the punches."

Putting together a presentation with slick visuals, theories, and secondary source market data is relatively easy. Substance materializes by entering the market, even on a small scale, and figuring out how to produce the revenue behind the slide deck promises and assumptions. "Don't spend time on fifty-page presentations," Jonathan says. Sound-Board, like their peers, looks for execution under real market conditions.

Talent

Execution only happens with talent. There is stuff that just needs to get done. When it comes to skills:

➤ The change maker (or their #2) must be able to sell.

➤ For a technology-based product, the change maker (or their #2) needs to create the technology.

Former iNovia Capital Partner Geoff Judge says, "If the CEO cannot sell, run."[7] The CEO is the chief revenue officer for a very long time. A technical CEO must bring in a partner whose core skill and passion is selling. And, it is hard to recruit great employees if you cannot sell.

Jonathan says, "Some people bring a product pitch for a solid business. But they have no sales background, and no technology skills. These founders bring very little to the party. Execution is ninety percent. The idea … eh. Later, as the company grows, sector knowledge takes on more importance."

The biggest risk to getting the business model right is making the right hires, deciding who is accountable for what, and how to lead and motivate. Know up front that you will make hiring mistakes, recognize the inevitability of doing so, and be fast about taking action.

Diversity still gets a lot of lip service and too little action, in spite of the evidence that gender and ethnically diverse teams deliver better results from early stage to legacy. People of different backgrounds and experiences coming together in a culture of open dialog and listening do a better job, plain and simple.

What story is told by the lineup of team photos under your company's "About Us" website tab or on corporate organization charts? Homogeneity of any type is a yellow flag.

Telling and selling the business model story

A business model is the story of serving a group of people who face a challenge. You see what is going on in these people's lives because you have stopped to listen to them. You have figured out a way to help them—touching their emotional needs and the day-in, day-out requirements to solve their problem. There are risks, obstacles, and breaks in the story.

Now you are the narrator of this story, and the audience you want to engage includes friends and family, investors, employees, and of course, users and buyers. Across this diverse group objectives will not always be consistent.

When you see the business model as a story and yourself as the narrator, you set yourself up to connect with—and persuade—the audience. Tell your story as a narrative that plugs into how the audience sees the world, not how you would like it to be.

Why does storytelling matter, anyway?

For starters, think about communications as a tool that helps you get what you want. How does it feel to have someone trying to sell you something with the stereotypical zeal of a sales person who won't take no for an answer? Haranguing potential customers with messaging about your product's greatness is a short-lived strategy. Much more welcoming is messaging that conveys a desire to serve and commitment to solving the user's problem.

Next, recognize that the power lies with your audience, not with you, to close a deal.

The secret is focus

Heather Thomas helps people build high growth businesses. Her track record at digital agency Critical Mass, where she led her team to a 70 percent win rate versus a category average of 25 percent, speaks for itself.[8] Heather's telling and selling tips:

> **1. Start with the audience and work back.** There are two angles to this advice—first, be hyper-focused on what kind of clients you want to serve. Says Heather, "During one period we got 250 inbound calls from prospective clients, we turned down 90 percent, but won 70 percent of those we pitched. We knew what we were looking for. We practiced the art of focus

and knew that to grow big we had to think small."

The team knew whom it *did not* want in a client as much as it knew whom it wanted. The same applies to choosing investors.

The second dimension is to have empathy for what people need, not what you want them to buy. Most people get nervous when delivering the pitch. But Heather says, "When you are in the room you may be nervous, but realize you are there to give your audience a gift—you are there for them. You are committed to them and to meeting their needs." Adopting that mindset reduces the pressure.

2. A well-framed and highly focused problem makes for a more memorable story. Figuring out the problem you are trying to solve is basic. Here's the replay of what this means in action in a dialog Heather had with a client. Watch how the problem Heather's client says he solves shifts from generic features —"We build websites and create banner ads"—to how he optimizes the checkout for luxury goods ecommerce sellers with sales impact:

Heather: "What do you do?'
Change maker: "We build websites and create banner ads."
H: "What are you good at? Experiential sites, transactional sites, or informational sites?"
C: "Transactional sites."
H: "So, are you a new house builder or a remodeler?"
C: "A remodeler."
H: "So, you are remodeling transactional websites. These include awareness, consideration, and checkout. What part of the process are you best at?"

C: "Well, we are really good at checkout. In fact, we optimize the checkout, and we know what conversion rates should be in the luxury goods space in particular."

H: "Great, then what you are saying is that your story focuses on why you are the people who refresh and refine the checkout process for luxury fashion brands. You do a diagnostic to figure out how you can help, then you do your magic."

Voila. There is quite a difference between redesigning websites—an expense whose value gets challenged by the CFO—versus improving the checkout experience for luxury fashion brands—which translates immediately into: "We make money for you."

Make the heart of your story how you solve the problem from your target audience's perspective. If you understand what will touch your audience you will stand out.

3. Think like a trial lawyer. When a trial lawyer goes to court, what are they thinking? "I have to make a persuasive argument to a skeptical audience that my case is right," says Heather. Sounds like what change makers have to achieve, too. She continues, "Work under the premise that there is always a competitor out there—opposing counsel whom you are up against." This means understanding not only selling messages, but as well what the barriers are.

4. What is holding you back may not be communications. I once led a team whose communications skills did not stack up. A communications expert ran a writers workshop, designed just for the team. Afterward she came by my office. "How did it go?" I asked. "Well," she replied, "here's the thing: sometimes bad writing is a sign of bad thinking."

A problematic story may be a symptom of poor market fit. Or the audience definition may require refinement. Or the offer itself may be weak. Listen for the substantive issues that can be fixed versus signals that it is time to pivot. Sometimes the best feedback is within the questions the audience asks in the course of listening to the story.

THE THREE Cs OF BUSINESS MODEL LINCHPINS

Capabilities:

The most useful business model capability in my personal toolkit is one my team crafted into a process driven by two questions we always had to answer to justify innovation investments to the CEO.

The process is simple, which is why it so useful. But don't be deceived. It can involve cycles of experimentation, demands critical thinking, and depends upon active listening.

The two-question construct: *Can you identify the unit profit model and then figure out how to scale? What would you have to believe for the business model to work?*

#1. The unit profit model

What is the unit of profit driving the business model? Is it customers? Accounts? Products? Transactions? Transaction size? Customer relationships? You should be able to answer if you know how the business works, and how you envision outcomes being created. Test assumptions to make sure you understand the unit of profit, and the connected drivers.

What will scale require? Can scale be achieved, given sales, marketing, and manufacturing assumptions? This means:

➤ Can the economics work?

➤ Is there an addressable market of people who need and have the means to buy?

➤ Can these people be reached with reasonable sales and marketing tactics, and reasonable investment?

The process works when you can identify and assemble the variables that together answer these questions, and test out each one precisely enough to support decisions—not more, not less. Examples of variables commonly on the list:

➤ User and buyer segments and sizes

➤ User and buyer behaviors—product purchase, usage, servicing, returns, replacements, repurchase, etc.

➤ Cost to acquire, activate, and retain

➤ Operating expense at scale per customer

➤ Manufacturing costs at scale per unit

➤ Fixed costs—and step functions that occur with volume increases

#2. What would you have to believe?

Answering this question is vital to judging unprecedented concepts, where no amount of intellect or expertise overcomes unknowns. Attempting to build a detailed spreadsheet with no factual basis for assumptions is an exercise in false precision. False precision kills concepts that may well have merit. A focus on "What would you have to believe?" avoids fruitless search for nonexistent data. It's a way to calm naysayers and those who dislike ambiguity.

Recommended approach:

➤ Make a list of the best guess revenue and expense lines driving the financials.

➤ Imagine three possible scenarios—high, medium, and low likelihood—distinguished by sales levels or customer base size achieved in the first few years. These are subjective choices. One option is to start with a scenario of 1 percent market share, as introduced in Chapter 1. What would you have to believe to achieve 1 percent? Does it feel within reach? Is it aggressively energizing or flat-out business suicide?

➤ Judge the likelihood of any of the three scenarios panning out by asking, "What would I have to believe?"

➤ Cover all aspects of the business model. Capture the list.

➤ Over time, with more real world experience, this qualitative assessment will shift to a more quantitative view—albeit one that will continue to rely on judgment, experimentation, and informed guesswork.

Connections:

The NAG effect

"NAG" is Heather Thomas's method to influence and win over an audience to the merits of a business model:

➤ Neutralize the competition's strengths;

➤ Stress the Advantages of the business model and offering;

➤ Guard against relative weaknesses.

Get focused by embracing the mental model of the trial lawyer. You are always up against some friction point. Take three steps to incorporate the NAG method into the story's substance and delivery:

1. Outline what the competition's strengths are and how you offset them.

2. Emphasize your advantage.

3. Explain how you preempt competitors' relative weaknesses.

Beware: Investors are wary of change makers who claim they have no competition. Show awareness and forethought about who else has a claim to the audience you seek to serve.

Connecting with your audience's mindset

A lot of energy goes into setting meeting dates and writing presentations. What drives the people you are trying to persuade? Professional labels—titles, roles, and brand affiliation—are good to know. And behind these labels there is also a person—an individual who has needs and wants, a life beyond your pitch, and who responds to empathy, including in B2B contexts.

Free or low-cost diagnostic tools are available to learn more about decision-making styles that affect selling and influencing. A basic search on phrases like "self-assessment tools for leadership behavior" will bring up a variety of such tools. These can be useful in identifying ways to increase impact as a leader and storyteller. As in any self-assessment, the value depends upon self-awareness, listening, and willingness to accept feedback. A mentor or other trusted adviser willing to provide guidance is invaluable.

Continue to use the user/buyer/payer/influencer model introduced in Chapter 1. Just view investors as the buyers of the business model.

Culture:

Cultural attributes for successful business model development include:

➤ **Intellectually curious,** seeking out insights upon which to base assumptions

➤ **Accepts and processes feedback** for iterating the business model

➤ **Flexible,** knowing when it is time to pivot

➤ **Collaborative,** ensuring different perspectives are voiced

➤ **Seeks diversity** because different perspectives drive innovation

➤ **Empathetic,** showing an understanding of others' feelings

Chapter summary

➤ A concept, however great, cannot become a business without a business model. And a business model cannot enable a concept without vision and purpose.

➤ A business model translates the prototype and the insights upon which it is based into the impacts on every aspect of operating and financial assumptions to launch and scale.

➤ Decisions about who you want to serve, plus the learning generated through in-market testing of the prototype, inform how the business model is refined—including sales and distribution strategy, components of the experience, pricing, talent profile, and organization design.

➤ Leaders who see failure as learning and enforce a culture of experimentation stand a stronger chance of creating viable business models. Don't blame the culture. Be the culture and lead.

➤ Building a business model that disrupts the incumbent model creates a hard-to-close gap between new and old.

➤ Beware of drifting away from achieving profitability within a reasonable timeframe, under reasonable assumptions.

➤ Investors evaluate the change maker (do they listen, accept feedback, own mistakes, and keep pace with the need to adapt?), execution strength, and ability to attract talent. The change maker must be able to tell their story and sell their product.

➤ After confidence in the change maker and the team, investors weigh heavily the strength and assumptions of the business model. This goes for private investors and senior executives deciding innovation investments inside an existing company.

➤ Bring in outsiders who see opportunities simply because they lack the baggage of being too close to your business or sector. Diversity and collaboration enable the business model to form and evolve.

➤ Convey the business model story as the narrative of vision, how you will deliver, and why people will be better off as a result. Know the audience for the story.

➤ Soft spots in the story may be forming for reasons besides communications. If the story doesn't feel strong, look back at the work begun in discovery and prototyping to see whether you have gone off course or missed an insight.

CHAPTER 6:
The Green-Light Moment

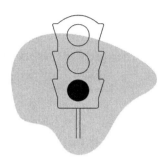

Hard work, persistence, and passion have helped you to get a lot done. Resourcefulness has enabled you to get insights about problems worth solving, cycle through prototypes, and rough out a business model. You've tapped into as many extra hours as you have been able to find in your days and nights. You have called in favors from friends, prevailed upon family members, and inspired colleagues.

The green-light moment is here. The market wants what you have created. You have the funds to move forward toward a launch.

First, take time to celebrate the achievement. Congratulate the people who have helped get here.

Second, recognize that your role continues to be a source of inspiration, builder of alliances, and obstacle eliminator. Not everyone is going to love what you are doing. Not everyone will automatically see the open space you see so readily. Sensitivity to your audience as you explain your vision on their terms, and how you separate the useful feedback from the naysaying still count.

The green-light moment is a time to pay attention to four priorities:

1. Purpose. Why you exist is your beacon.

2. People. Without the right moves on people—attracting, selecting, and motivating talent who can deliver in the right roles within your culture—nothing else matters. So we will start here.

3. Strategy. Without a strategy—a documented articulation of where you are heading, how you envision getting there, and why—the best talent will be compromised. Strategy is the basis for execution.

4. Execution. Implementing in line with vision and purpose means being ready to deal with whatever surprises occur along the way.

Focus has been on living and breathing product, product, product, putting up enough support structure to get by with minimal resources and all-consuming effort.

Now is the time to regroup as your role changes from doer of everything or most things, to doer of many things, as well as leader, coach, and orchestra conductor of a larger, more complex effort.

PEOPLE

Getting the right people in

Demonstrate every day that you are running relentlessly toward success to attract and win people over to your cause. Show your commitment to taking the team along with you. Reinforce you are serious with tangible proof.

You may have or lack administrative and process support to manage people, but it is your job alone to set the bar on talent. You have hustled for dollars and technology. Now, find and engage the best people.

Assessing hires by learning about competencies

Interviewing and assessing candidates is a learned skill. Seek all guidance on how to be an effective interviewer. Know and set the expectation that the interview experience is also the time to sell the role and the company.

Competency-based interviewing is a technique that zeros in on how a person has used specific skills to solve problems in the past. The goal is to encourage the candidate to share examples illustrating how they felt and acted in real life. A quick search of the term "competency-based interviewing" will net good, free resources if you don't have access to formal training.

This technique follows two basics:

1. **"Tell me about a time when ..."** This question gets to specific examples of how a candidate has demonstrated a sought-after skill. Example: "Tell me about a time when you worked through conflicting or ambiguous data to make a decision." Or, "Tell me about a time when you implemented an unexpected change in direction with no time to spare." Probe: "And then what did you do?" "What did you say during the meeting?" "How did you feel?" "How did others respond?" Dig until you can envision what actually happened.

2. **Avoid asking, "What would you do ...?"** This lead-in to any question invites conjecture, which is worthless. Answers that are conceptually sound but not linked to behavior do not

prove ability. Smart people know what to say and generate the right answer whether they are able to pull off what they are describing or not. It is too easy for a candidate to say the right stuff (and, by the way, fully believe it) but not know how to roll up their sleeves and make it happen.

(To get double-duty from these basics, use them in discovery as well.)

Avoid the biggest hiring mistakes:

➤ **Bringing in people who are just like you**. Homogeneity harms innovation. Find team members who complement expertise and increase execution capacity. The right people may be those who make you uncomfortable, stirring debate about approaches that would not have occurred to you.

➤ **Under- or over-hiring expertise**. Under-hiring shows up when a person lacking the skills, leadership, and gravitas to be effective under pressure cannot produce or quantify results beyond low-level tactics. Give stretch assignments, but how much stretch is a matter of judgment. Over-hiring can be deadly too. Have you ever been in a role where you felt underutilized and didn't see growth on the horizon? When hiring decisions involve tradeoffs, know why you are under- or over-hiring, be clear about expectations, and deliver on your end of the deal.

➤ **Hiring for skill alone, without assessing culture fit and leadership**. On a small team even a single misfire has consequences. Can people not just stomach, but thrive on the roller coaster ride from concept to execution? Hire for fit with values so you can count on everyone to exercise consistent judgment.

➤ **Compromising.** You are better off having one really great person than a few who are just okay. Buy great part-time or interim talent, be patient, and network.

➤ **Poorly framing roles.** The challenge: learning how to define roles, design the organization, and create processes for how the work gets done tend to happen someplace between real time and seat of the pants. Consult people whose expertise is the basis for good counsel. Whatever you do, don't throw a great person under the bus because of your failures to set them up to succeed.

➤ **Misreading people's skills and motivations.** A founder shared the story that she had to spend months resolving a potential regulatory showstopper resulting from cofounder misrepresentations in SEC filings. A background check would have preempted the problem. Another founder was informed the day after closing a seed round that his cofounder—and most expert developer—was jumping ship. Luckily, both founders were able to keep efforts from unraveling. Do a thorough due diligence on every candidate, starting with potential cofounders, to avoid these situations.

Be honest about how you assess people and confront your own biases. If you believe someone has the skills but "doesn't fit" with the culture, are you rationalizing away the fact that they are different? If you think someone is overqualified, is the truth that you are uncomfortable bringing on board someone who is older, has more degrees, or has had bigger titles or more experience than you?

Another angle on hiring: Hire people who know the things that you don't know, and who like to do the things that you prefer not to do.

Clear responsibilities, strong players

A CEO once told me his theory of hiring: "Just remember, one of three hires you make is likely a mistake. The trick is to figure out who that one is, and take action."

Whether this ratio is right or not, firing people is at the bottom of the list of things anyone likes to do. Just keep in mind, as you delay tough people decisions, everyone else holds you accountable to act— now. They are just not telling you. Acting quickly and respectfully signals that you care, value the team's efforts, and can carry out the right decisions, however tough.

Texas-based Wholesome Sweeteners' original business was as a provider of organic sweeteners to food manufacturers. New investors wanted the company to pursue a retail strategy, raising new requirements for talent, organization design, and leadership.

Olu Beck took on the role as Wholesome's CEO to relaunch the company, following a career at Mars Inc., Johnson & Johnson, and running her eponymous consulting firm. Olu's first ninety days centered on three priorities: establishing the vision, evaluating the people, and assessing the culture. Within those first three months, she made tough calls on senior leadership changes. But, she says, "It wasn't willy-nilly."[1] She first invested in user insights to understand consumer needs and then to craft a compelling vision and strategy that drove execution choices. The vision and strategy provided the template for all aspects of the business, including priorities, structure, roles, and responsibilities.

Getting the people decisions right initiates a virtuous cycle. Great people make great things happen. When other great prospective team members see the progress, more of the right people want to join and contribute.

Mark Walsh, former head of the Office of Innovation and Investment for the United States Small Business Administration, and an entrepreneur and private sector executive, does not hesitate to voice his views. He says, "People issues are *the* issue. A team that is working well together and is functioning and productive—that is the team that will win. It isn't about technology. Strategy and execution come down to the people."[2]

STRATEGY

Strategy is where execution begins. Done right, strategy encompasses not only conceptual logic and analyses, but also how execution will happen. Strategy answers four questions:

1. **The starting point**: Where are you now?

2. **The destination**: Where do you want to be?

3. **The route**: How do you anticipate getting there?

4. **The rationale**: Why does any of this matter?

As basic as these questions are, lots of teams gathered around lots of whiteboards argue they don't have time for strategy. These teams somehow see strategy as dispensable, a diversion from action. In the name of speed, they jump to a schedule of tasks. I've even known leaders who categorize as "strategic" those projects that cannot yet be quantified. Red flag. A strategy is only a strategy if it aims toward a destination. The destination may turn out to be different, but a stake in the ground is essential. And of course, the route will change many times.

Strategy assures delivery of results. No need for fancy consultants or fancy documents. Take the Version 1.0 approach, and iterate over time.

➤ **The Two Where's.** The answers to the now and later questions of *where* set context for smart decisions. Context motivates people and costs nothing. The starting point and destination are already in the business model metrics. Whether you are at a startup or grown-up company, these two questions demand answers.

➤ **The How.** The execution plan turns out to be the hardest of the four elements to nail. Defining *how* means getting from the pages of the pitch into the real world where things get complicated. The best plans lead to a finish line because of the team's ability to adapt on the fly.

➤ **The Why.** Knowing *why* accelerates decisions and assures consistency without micromanagement. Being clear and open about "why" is much more effective than authoritarian leadership if you want to attract and retain people who are wired for innovation.

Strategy has stepping-stones between insights, purpose, and execution. For the many decisions that cannot be predetermined, strategy empowers the business builder and their team to operate with a shared view of the destination and the guideposts to get there.

Anticipating Plan B

President Dwight D. Eisenhower gets credit for having said, "Plans are worthless, but planning is everything." Doubtful that Ike didn't value strategy. Rather, his words acknowledge that no matter how robust the plans they are going to be revised by reality.

Ambiguity and nonlinear progress are innovation constants. So be ready to summon Plan B at all times.

Eisenhower made his comments in 1957—a different era—to leaders whose role was handling national emergencies. He said, "When you are planning for an emergency you must start with this one thing: the very definition of 'emergency' is that it is unexpected, therefore it is not going to happen the way you are planning."[3]

Change makers are unlikely to run into anything on the order of a national crisis affecting their plans, but the unexpected lies ahead. Plan B people either have back-pocket options or are able to produce them in no time. That's because they are good at:

➤ Listening

➤ Facing facts

➤ Balancing internal and external focus

➤ Uncovering new insight

➤ Framing the problem to be solved

➤ Decision-making at a brisk pace

➤ Learning and reflecting

➤ Being rational and empathetic

Plan B is where the change maker's passion aligns with execution. But sometimes perceptions are different. Mark Walsh sees a risk that comes with Plan B: Investors buy into a vision then misread a proactive Plan B as wavering commitment to Plan A. Mark says, "VCs expect complete dedication to the point where they act like they see Plan B as a lack of faith. Of course, then when things do go wrong, the founder gets blamed if he is without Plan B."

At Wholesome Sweeteners, Olu Beck's planning priorities encompassed two issues beyond her control. Both demanded Plan B anticipation. First, what if government trade policy changed, affecting dependencies for raw materials imports and finished product exports? Second, what if some new competitor entered with a significant strategic advantage? Intensifying interest in the organic foods category could mean unpredictable moves by startups and incumbents.

Rick Greenberg is on his third startup, having already built Kepler Group into an *Inc.* 500 provider of marketing analytics. He sees a planning mindset as essential to value and growth. Rick says, "In the old days we let the market lead us toward incremental innovation. Now we think ahead of the market and aim to rapidly react to customers, investors, competitors, and employees."[4]

The bottom line is that strategy and planning drive:

➤ How or whether the vision is achieved

➤ The ability to surface issues proactively, and adapt to the unexpected

➤ Focus on priorities, while setting aside what may be interesting but distracting

➤ Communications and alignment

EXECUTION

Execution takes time. And every change maker faces unforgiving pressure to move faster. Weeks are compressed into days, months into weeks, and years into months. The constant demand is to execute, get the product out, and achieve results. Otherwise, run the risk of losing support from investors and employees, and ceding to competitors the opportunity you have worked so hard to define.

Time compression creates energy and forces progress, but without strategy and planning, speedy execution alone generates chaos.

Do you enjoy execution, and are you good at it?

Remember to assess your own competencies as you move ahead on people decisions. What role will you play? This is a good time to be clear on where and how you can contribute the most, and where you should stay out of the way. Maybe you are the kind of person who wants to come up with a concept and keep everyone focused on the end game, but have someone else sweat the details. Or is the purpose powering the company so personal that you are not comfortable with anyone else assuming the lead role?

Know who you are and who you are not. Know for sure that trying to prove that you can do it all will prove disastrous. Now that it is time to bring your vision to life, size up your own capacity to execute and find ways to offset shortfalls.

Serial entrepreneur Paolo Gaudiano has embarked on a mission to revolutionize how people think about diversity and inclusion, and what they do about it. To achieve this goal, he founded the Initiative for the Quantitative Studies of Diversity and Inclusion (QSDI) at the City College of New York, and also launched "diversity tech" company Aleria.

As he builds this venture, Paolo is clear on where he fits in. He says, "I always had an allergic reaction to the idea of a business plan. I am the idea guy. For me, the vexing problem has been to find operating executives for my companies who complement me from a practical perspective but are also my twin from a values perspective."[5]

If the view from the outside is that things are going great, it's unlikely that is because the change maker is doing it all on their own. Chances are that they are beating the execution odds by making the right hires and leading non-hierarchically. And they have attracted super-competent people who are equally committed to the vision, who round out the team's capabilities, and who work together.

So don't try to convince yourself or others that you personally are the all-in-one solution. It's tough to be both the early stage visionary and the operator who scales the business. The larger the organization, the harder it is to remain the visionary *and* hold people's feet to the fire. Lots of times when a change maker seems to be doing both, the truth is that alongside them is a great number two. Think about the complementary relationships between Mark Zuckerberg and Sheryl Sandberg, or Larry Ellison and Ray Lane.

Back in earlier days of fax machine, copier, printer, and scanner, the all-in-one solution looked like the way to go. All-in-one can mean not being terribly good at the individual features.

Knowing yourself puts you in the position to make assets out of personal traits that might otherwise work against you. Paolo says, "My recalcitrance about details has probably helped when it comes to execution." Huh? People like Paolo focus on the vision, and because he prefers not to immerse in the details he is more flexible about letting others get things done.

Rick Greenberg speaks with the authority and knowledge of someone who has been there and done it. He shared a story about a friend who sought his advice about creating a business. Rick says, "I told him point-blank I didn't think he could succeed. He could not see that this isn't a field of dreams where you build it and people come to your door. He didn't realize he would have to face failures every day, and still keep executing."

Putting on the operator hat means being a role model for:

➤ **Attitude.** Absorbing failure and learning from it. Seeing progress over setbacks.

➤ **Courage.** Rick says, "Although we are now a scale business, there are still daily bumps in the road where I absorb the blows."

➤ **Purpose.** Knowing the North Star and staying true to it— an unwavering commitment to the special way the brand generates value.

➤ **Progress.** Getting points on the board early, demonstrating incremental advances.

➤ **Culture.** Defining and establishing the environment, values, principles, and behaviors—the ways and means that drive all of the "how's."

Are you ready to listen so you can lead?

Lots of people have made the leap from concept and pitch to launch and scale. Be smart about your advisers. You cannot listen to everyone. And if you are not resolute about purpose, your head will spin from all the conflicting advice. Or you will second-guess yourself as you hear tales of what can go wrong, of how hard the journey is, of the moments of near failure.

Foundations for being a good 360-degree listener:

➤ Walking the tightrope of being stubborn *and* open-minded.

➤ Believing in your vision and yourself, while also admitting you will always have a lot to learn. Confess to ignorance and be up front when you are wrong.

➤ Being available to the team for rapid problem solving.

➤ Resolving conflicts so they don't become bigger and harder.

➤ Knowing when to decide and act—when good enough is good enough.

➤ Encouraging the focus-forcing question: What do we really need to accomplish right now to move ahead?

➤ Remembering "why." Remind yourself, "This is what I am trying to achieve." Write it on a note to tape to the side of your computer screen, or on a piece of paper to keep in your wallet.

Understand what's in it for each member of the team

Your purpose is amazing. What are you doing to ensure your team sees what's in it for them? The "WIFM principle"—what's in it for me—is not about cynicism or self-interest at others' expense. We all want to take care of ourselves and our loved ones. We evaluate personal plusses and minuses, and are more motivated when the weighting is one that feels favorable, whether overtly or subconsciously. Behavioral economic theory finds that as a species we overweight risk relative to reward.[6] An upside cannot be too clear, nor can it be over-communicated.

Rick Greenberg's philosophy about sustaining a strong employee WIFM *sounds* unremarkable: treat people with respect and assure they are motivated and able to do great work. What is remarkable is that he adheres to this philosophy. He knows success depends upon execution. Execution depends upon people's engagement. And their engagement depends upon his leadership.

Have you ever fired a client to protect your culture and your team? Rick has. He says, "We had to. We found ourselves in a classically poisoned agency-client relationship, a constant negative cycle that was destroying our ability to scale the business because of the impact on our people." Staying true to what the leadership team wants to stand for has made Kepler Group one of the highest-rated companies on Glassdoor.

Laurel Blatchford is senior vice president and chief program officer at Enterprise Community Partners. Enterprise is a national nonprofit organization providing capital, programmatic innovation, and policy support to the affordable housing and community development sector. Laurel takes a consistent view to that of corporate leaders: providing a compelling WIFM is all about knowing where people need support and ensuring they get it.[7] For one person, what matters may be help navigating relationships—the internal organization or the sector ecosystem. Another person may be strong on day-to-day routine but less effective handling the unexpected. Some people run straight into complexity and ambiguity, others prefer structure. Most people can be good at many things—just not everything—depending upon the situation.

Figure out the fit between what is required not just based on each person's skill, but also on their motivation to get the job done.

Mark Walsh says, "If people don't believe in what you are telling them or want to be part of the journey, you are bound to fail."

Communicate to drive execution

The change maker knows where they are heading and has to make sure everyone else sees the path and end game. Nothing will pass the green light without communications that are two-way, ongoing, transparent, and constructive.

Committing the strategy to writing will test and improve thought clarity. Use conversations about the strategy to push issues to the surface, build buy-in, take advantage of what other people know and have experienced, and align resources with actions that matter. If you are working (at least for now) as a soloist, don't settle for having it all inside your head. You will help yourself by writing down the strategy—all four elements—and debating the framework with mentors and advisers.

Rick Greenberg says, "There is one in a million leader who can listen to no one—maybe that one in our generation was Steve Jobs." Founders can fall into the "I am right, I am the visionary, therefore I know" trap. Sometimes that works. You may have to say, "There's no time for debate." But that is a limited-utility tactic.

To the extent you listen, you gain or lose credibility, affecting others' will to listen to you. Mark Walsh has worked in many different organization cultures. His listening tactics have been consistent and have allowed him to test and boost team readiness to execute. Here's how he does it:

➤ **Forms small groups.** Roundtable lunches get people out of the daily structure of work. In a big place, this takes multiple sessions.

➤ **Gathers around food.** Such meetings open up communications and lower rank and role barriers.

➤ **Breaks the ice.** Encouraging introductions. Even on small teams, people often don't know each other and may not be aware of what colleagues are working on.

➤ **Humanizes himself.** Getting beyond name, rank, and serial number lets people see you as a whole person.

➤ **Shares the vision and strategy.** Answering in relatable language the four questions comprising the strategy, with passion, gets people engaged.

➤ **Assesses what's going on within the team.** The team's enthusiasm and thoughtful feedback signal the bedrock is in place to execute. Mark follows up on warning flags—when he hears silence or party-line comments like, "Hey, great idea."

Do you feel as though all you do is repeat yourself? Great, if you are asking a team to execute something big, new, and bold. People working in these situations are justified in needing over-the-top reminders. Why are they being asked to achieve the impossible? Why should they work so hard and take on risk?

Being heard is a profound human need. So is providing context— *why* is the issue of the day a priority, not just *what* needs to get done today. It's unlikely that the people you must convince and engage are mind readers. Keep everyone in the game by communicating proactively, frequently, repeatedly, and in multiple channels and formats.

Fostering a culture of execution for results

Research undertaken at Google identified five team characteristics associated with strengthening a delivery-oriented culture of innovation:[8]

1. Dependability. Work is completed on time, in line with expectations.

2. Structure and clarity. Clear goals and roles are in place.

3. Meaning. People gain personal significance through their work.

4. Impact. The work has purpose and affects the greater good.

5. Psychological safety. People are comfortable taking risks and allowing themselves to be vulnerable.

How can you tell whether these conditions are present? People will be open. Even on their own time, they will go beyond what is required. They will buy into the notion that failure is learning, so they take risks. They ask questions, learn, and demonstrate accountability.

The environment you create will attract and sustain people who want to be in your kind of culture, good or bad. The culture of every organization is unique to that place. So don't try to make your culture like someone else's. Learn from others, seek role models, but know who you are. Be sensitive to how culture drives the talent you will land and their effectiveness.

THE THREE Cs OF THE GREEN-LIGHT MOMENT

Capabilities:

Strategy framework

The goal of creating a strategy document is not cool PowerPoint slides, so don't make a project out of creating a presentation. Use a simple template such as the one included here to frame answers to the four questions of strategy. Developing the answers is a great topic for a work session to get the benefit of collaboration.

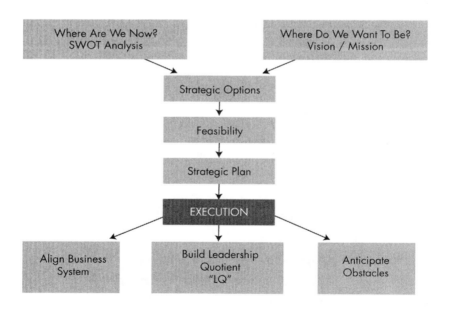

Prioritizing execution: The effort-to-impact matrix

Use this matrix to facilitate choosing priorities. Use it on your own to create a relative mapping of a burdensome to-do list. Even better, use it as the anchor for team decisions.

The quality of the mapping depends upon the assumptions. The goal is to steer resources toward the highest-impact/least-effort activities, and eliminate those that score high effort but low impact.

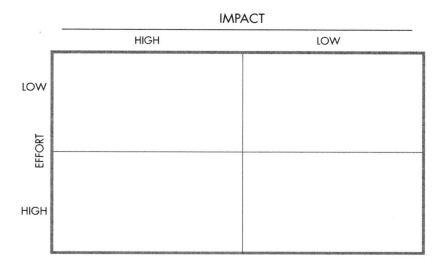

Creating a look-back log to retain and apply learning

As children we are taught to learn from our mistakes. More enlightened organizations see learning as the value harvested from failure. A culture in which failure is seen as learning and not a punitive event is one where people will be comfortable maintaining a look-back log.

This can be a simple running table reviewed for the latest updates in short, periodic team meetings. Columns capture:

➤ What impeded me?

➤ What was within/outside my control?

➤ What was predictable or not?

➤ What did we do about it?

➤ What did we learn and what should we remember for the future?

➤ What was the outcome?

Increase people's effectiveness by flexing to their learning styles

People learn differently. Why does this matter? Learning happens non-stop on a team delivering innovation. Tune in to people's preferences for absorbing and processing information, insights, and data. Then adapt your own behavior to support their preferences.

I became interested in the impact of learning styles on effective performance during my children's middle school years, and started to think about how these principles apply at work. Start by identifying who among your team and other connections are:

➤ **Visual learners:** People who respond to images and pictures versus words and spreadsheets.

➤ **Verbal learners:** People who prefer words—text and narrative—whether in speech or in writing.

➤ **Aural learners:** People who want to hear from you versus reading reports or transcripts.

➤ **Data-oriented learners:** People who learn more effectively through numbers and systems.

➤ **Real-time learners:** People who benefit from group discussion to work through ideas, insights, and data, and will provide their input there and then.

➤ **Ahead-of-time learners:** People who want to get familiar with whatever the content is, and mull it over before the meeting.

Use active listening skills to determine individuals' learning styles, just by observing behavior and how people react to your communications.

➤ What kind of materials do team members gravitate toward? Format accordingly.

➤ Do people want to review everything at the meeting, read in advance, or get back to you later? Distribute what you've got to support preferences.

➤ Are you working with a group whose individual styles vary? Consider formatting the same information multiple ways—images, charts, and text. Send everything out in advance. For super-important matters, even offer to review information one-on-one prior to key group decision-making sessions.

To the extent the team understands and adapts to each other's learning styles, understanding and collaboration—and execution effectiveness—will improve.

Connections:

Additional opportunities for strategic networking

Chapter 3 introduced strategic networking as one of the Three Cs of resourcefulness. Networking is being reintroduced here because well-cared-for relationships supercharge efforts to transition from seeding to scaling. Getting from idea to execution, or problem to solution, may be only a phone call or cup of coffee away. Costly unforced errors can be circumvented with just a small piece of sought-out advice.

It's surprising that there are people out there who still narrowly associate networking with a job search. Take a wider view of networking and you will see results. Networking saves time. And the time invested has high personal ROI.

A great network includes at least two kinds of people: people who always have ideas about helpful resources, and people who have knowledge and information they like to share. Persistent takers may get what they want—an introduction, an email address, a short answer to a question, a one-way transaction—but they will not get beyond the superficial.

Who you know and how skilled you are at forming and tapping into relationships surpasses technical skill when you suddenly must be smart about the expanding list of topics that are part of scaling, and that go well beyond domain expertise.

Stay committed to a routine even when the workload feels relentless. Those moments may be most when a conversation with the right person lifts the burden.

With nurturing, relationships sprout and grow. Network members may one day come to your rescue or you to theirs. So many of such instances are serendipitous, and cannot be planned.

Ongoing connections also alleviate the isolation that comes with being on an innovation edge.

Culture:

Cultural attributes for a successful green-light moment include:

➤ **Driven by metrics** that are grounded in common sense

➤ **Transparent** about what success requires, acknowledges mistakes, and gives feedback

➤ **Supportive of taking risks** to push the boundaries for learning and execution

➤ **Values and principles based,** making tough trade-offs ethically and thoughtfully

➤ **Optimistic** and hopeful even under pressure

➤ **Indefatigable** exuding speed, focus, and flexibility

Chapter summary

➤ People, strategy, and execution are the three essentials of the green-light moment where attention is on moving toward launching and scaling.

➤ Without the right people and culture, nothing else matters.

➤ Strategy addresses four questions: Where are we now? Where are we heading? How will we get there? Why are we creating the innovation?

➤ The execution path detailing "how" is core to the strategy. Advancing Plan B as an element of strategy anticipates the options for dealing with the unexpected.

➤ Know who you are, be honest about your strengths, and enlist people who complement you.

➤ Avoid common hiring mistakes: seek diversity versus people like you, avoid under- or over-hiring or otherwise compromising on talent decisions.

➤ Assess people by learning about how they have behaved in situations that can shed light on what they do and how they do it.

➤ Relationships in your network are sources of solutions to problems.

➤ Few people can read minds, so keep everyone engaged and informed by being a two-way communicator. Recognize and convey what's in it for them.

PART III:
SCALING

"The last 10 percent it takes to launch something
takes as much energy as the first 90 percent."
Rob Kalin, founder, Etsy[1]

"See things in the present even if they are in the future."
Larry Ellison, cofounder, Oracle[2]

By now, people, strategy, and execution are redirected from concept, prototyping, and validation to deliver the real thing. How you allocate time and effort to the demands of your fledgling product or business is shifting to make it in the market.

Seeking revealed the beginnings of ideas to explore and develop by encouraging looking around, playing with ideas, and building early models. Seeking required observing people, shaping hypotheses and then tossing those hypotheses aside for new ones. The goal was to find problems big and meaningful enough to solve.

Seeding's goal was to apply early insights to define viable solutions with a large enough market of users, based on back-of-the-envelope precision. Prototypes, a business model, and data gelled into the pitch for resources, and informed a strategy including how to execute.

To scale, attention shifts to driving sales, attracting users and buyers, and earning loyalty, engagement, and referrals. The pressure is on to figure out how to hit the numbers, and understand where you were right or under- or overestimated. Business model expectations were based on best guess assumptions, some data, and lots of hypotheses.

Scaling expands requirements. Commitments to defining and delivering on user needs, iterating quickly, and aligning resources do not stop. You are juggling balls and spinning plates. To keep everything in the air, *Scaling* offers guidance, stories, concepts and tools for the last three pieces of the framework:

1. **Launch.** Business model expectations will be pushed harder, tested, proven or disproven, expanded, and refined. What does a successful launch look like? What does it take to be a launch leader? They are likely the change maker, but may be someone stepping in with leadership and execution

capabilities to grow in market *and* continue to innovate. Why do launches fail and how can pitfalls be avoided? What learning can be drawn from businesses where you might not have guessed there are relevant lessons?

2. Testing and experimentation. The needs for agility and iteration do not end. Testing and experimentation are a mindset, not just skills or steps in a process. What happens post-launch? How do the habits of ongoing learning, challenging norms, and trial-and-error pursuits live when hitting the numbers becomes the daily priority? What does a test-and-learn culture look like?

3. Anticipating and adapting. No business sits still. Leaders who once seemed like unstoppable winners lose when they fail to see success as temporary. What once made them great—seizing upon an insight ignored by incumbents—is no longer enough. Marketplace successes stay on top when leaders anticipate and adapt. They shape the next horizon line.

Scale used to mean big absolute size. Standards for scale still include yardsticks of sales, revenue, and profits. These results were enabled by complex infrastructure. But traditional requirements to scale a customer base have fallen away. And, in a world where extreme personalization is technologically possible (and increasingly expected), big infrastructure can turn out to be a burden. There is no longer a best definition for how big the infrastructure should be—except, perhaps, no bigger than necessary, and as small as possible.

Can entire sectors transform? Can all stakeholders share innovation successes? Or do we live in a winner-take-all world? Entire predigital sectors are disappearing. What will the next era of economic and social development look like? How can change makers shape positive outcomes for society at large?

CHAPTER 7

Launch

A successful entrepreneur tried to convince me that the notion of launching is out of step with startups' iterative methods. "Startups are not the audience for this conversation," he said. I respectfully disagree. There is a point of lift off, when the goal is a steep adoption curve. Sales must materialize at startup and grown-up companies.

Defining launch

Launch is when a team shifts efforts toward delivering product at the scale of results projected in the business model. It is when users expect the product to be available and functional, for platforms to work and customer service to be responsive.

Startup or grown-up business, you are ready to launch when you have crossed over from low-volume beta testing to having earned the capital for expanded sales and marketing. The growing team is implementing, moving from paper-and-tape models—metaphorical or real—to manufacturing lines with stable production. Information security protocols reflect prime-time standards. Materials sourcing and delivery teams are gearing up for volume and quality.

So call it launch. Call it roll-out. Call it expansion. It may just feel like the next bigger iteration. Or it may be the "big bang." You may be running so quickly that you only realize in retrospect when the shift into launch gear happened. This is a new push requiring more diverse skills, set in place during your green-light moment, and carrying opportunities and risks not requiring attention until now.

Take the case of a potential blockbuster drug—the culmination of years of research and development and regulatory approvals. To enable launch, sales, marketing, manufacturing, and distribution are set up based upon best-case regulatory approval and trial scenarios. Millions of dollars are invested. Decision makers live with the possibility of an eleventh-hour no-go.

Or take the case of a retail footwear brand, where the race is on to get the next high fashion sneaker into stores. Over forty new products launch every week. The race is nonstop just to keep up with taste trends.[1]

Whether a new product, a product extension, a new business line, or a whole new entity, launches share common traits. Those assumptions plugged into the business model spreadsheet? Now is the time to make them real.

Big public launch failures make headlines. And there is plenty to report on. An online search of "biggest product flops" leads off with Ford's Edsel, whose failure was so spectacular that the name came to stand for massive product failure.[2]

Consider as you set launch plans some of the biggest risks:

➤ Misses on choosing the right people to scale the business, and setting talent up to succeed;

➤ Failing to connect operational decisions to the business model;

➤ Losing sight of the market need that once looked certain.

Launch questions to keep on your radar

Are you on track to pass the 10x test?

Founder Peter Thiel has advocated that to succeed commercially, an innovation must be ten times better than whatever the user currently has available.[3]

Ten times better means a *dramatically* better alternative. The 10x test may be met during beta testing. But now, execution must ensure wallets open, and product is snapped up at the expense of yesterday's solution.

Warning: A low price launch message is tough to sustain. Is promotional pricing a reasonable tactic to help attract attention? Or is it a cover-up for failing the 10x test? Is what looked convincing as a prototype now less compelling?

Examine whether:

➤ User reaction to prototypes was overestimated because of test design;

➤ The team fell in love with its own idea, blocking its ability to understand market feedback;

➤ The concept was diminished with each implementation challenge;

➤ User needs have changed faster than your ability to get to market.

Are you prepared to meet the launch expectations you have set?

Look back. What expectations were created by beta results, market analyses, and business model assumptions?

Expectations grow as production, sales, and marketing efforts expand. Conflicting expectations coexist. The business will be amazing and new ... and things will be messy. There will be stops and starts, lots of stuff flying around, at the same time as media commitments are being made, while revenue projections and potential risks grow.

And you created believers by passionately selling your concept and inspiring others with your purpose.

Is the team too focused?

Someplace within the organizations of grown-up brands sit new product development teams or some other form of innovation units. While the rest of the organization is delivering short-term financial commitments, these people are defining new horizons. Dedicating resources to figuring out what's next makes sense. But, singular dedication to launching new products or businesses can have unintended consequences.

What's the problem? If a team's reason for being is to launch new products, what if they cannot find winners? What if they cannot generate new income streams, or attract the right customers? Given the low success rate of new products, most efforts will *not* deliver on expectations. It's understandable that once a team is vested in an idea, sells everyone, and consumes resources, it's extraordinarily difficult to let go of a launch already underway.

A division president for a global brand captures the issue when he says, "At the very early stage there probably wasn't a viable new idea. But someone was told they worked on developing new products. That meant they had to produce new stuff. It's hard to find worthy new ideas. To get something out the door pressure builds to move ahead with something, even if mediocre."

Three consequences of an innovation silo:

➤ The dedicated team makes installation of a process the thing for which they expect to be rewarded. Set off on their own, these smart, skilled people lose sight of why they are being paid: to create great new businesses that fulfill market needs. They get lost in the "how" of innovation, and are not accountable for outcomes.

➤ The "ugly baby" syndrome takes hold. A concept users love is gradually diminished. Tradeoffs chip off bits and pieces of what users are looking for, to get past internal obstacles. The team loses sight of the original solution. But they stuck with this baby so they have to love it. After all, how many times have you ever heard anyone say a baby is ugly, especially when it is their own creation?

➤ The rest of the organization is impacted. The positive: rank-and-file employees know the world is changing, and sigh with relief because executives see the light. The unintended consequences? The innovation team is taking care of innovation, so no one else needs to worry. Or others are resentful. They want to be involved and are not given the opportunity. The c-suite has a reaction all its own. Without being put on a collective hook for innovation results, internal politics compromise the innovation agenda. Capital and attention are eventually diverted back to short-term priorities associated with familiar, silo metrics.

Still, the number of innovation labs has been on the rise.[4] Boards and CEOs acknowledge that innovation is fundamental to sustained relevance. They see that mature business units smother innovation. The hope is that organizational or geographic isolation will be liberating.

Of course for true startups, heads-down focus also causes fallout—there is so much to be done, keeping all balls in the air and staying connected to user needs is hard. The clock is running based on cash burn, and tolerance for eating ramen noodles three times a day is declining. Investors abandon ventures perceived as unlikely to become one of the few portfolio winners. This Darwinian process short circuits businesses and assures they will not go the distance.

Are you getting ready for what scale means?

In the case of product manufacturing—say, a chemical compound like a new drug—active ingredients may be in short supply, even rare. Perhaps such compounds can only be procured in sufficient quantity from a far-away supplier. Perhaps, for a new product, textiles are produced in one location, and are assembled elsewhere. Or prototype development happened locally, overseen by founders. Now, to hit unit costs production moves to a vendor located elsewhere.

Take the launch of the American Express Blue Card, an early example of a payment product designed by a grown-up brand for millennial users.

Former American Express executive Richard Quigley led the team that brought Blue to market.[5] The card launched as the first mass issued clear credit card. It contained an embedded smart microchip—at a time when this technology was not yet a U.S. standard.

Everything was ready—advertising produced, media purchased, and the organization operating in high gear. Plastics were coming off the assembly line. But something crazy happened. The standard process was to produce cards in batches of a hundred. A sensor "knew" that when the hundredth card broke through a laser beam, the batch was complete. "Because the card was clear," Richard says, "the laser beam was going *through* the plastic, so production was not stopping. Plastics were flying all over the place."

A workaround resolved the production problem, by relying upon the weight of the batch, rather than the laser beam. Then, an engineer flagged another problem, this time one that could directly impact customers. It turned out ATMs, an essential access point, also relied upon laser beams to recognize a card had been inserted.

Serendipity, communications, and fast decisions helped avoid the failure of a basic product feature. Launches do not always encounter such good luck. Nurturing the right cultural conditions with the right talent increases the odds.

What launch leadership qualities matter most?

Cheer for the launch leader who is:

➤ **Highly adaptable whether** in fluid circumstances or when faced with challenges.

➤ **A creative problem solver and critical thinker** who looks beyond norms for answers. They do not have all the answers; they are able to get the best from the team or know where else to go.

➤ **Focused on a shared view of launch success** that keeps the team together.

➤ **A clear communicator.** The more unprecedented the horizon line, the harder to grasp. Making the view more visible helps everyone.

➤ **Decisive, opting for speed.** In his 2016 shareholder letter, Jeff Bezos points out that 70 percent of the information is the ideal amount to inform a decision.[6] Trends don't wait. Fashion veteran Kate Kibler says, "Have a strong point of view about what you want the customer to get behind."[7]

➤ **Calm, putting team members at ease.** Things go wrong especially under pressure. The launch leader sustains the belief that things can get back on track, which becomes a self-fulfilling prophecy. Yes, we all know screamers—they flame out, and are terrible role models.

➤ **Accountable.** At grown-up companies, launch leaders must avoid celebrating adherence to process. Reminder: process is not the thing that matters. The launch has to prove that the product meets market needs.

➤ **An ego-in-check person.** They seek out the best partners to advance out-of-the-box launch strategies. They earn internal support and advocacy.

The launch leader is nimble. They adapt plans on a dime and marshal people and resources. They maintain an open culture motivating everyone to chip in what they know. They put people at ease with never having all of the facts. They have assembled a team eager to contribute and win.

What goes into establishing market awareness?

The marketing plan goal is to maximize launch impact. Producing a great marketing plan is tough. Why? For starters, marketing has always been misunderstood. It relies upon a mixture of financial and non-financial metrics. It is undergoing rapid disruption and reinvention.

Be aware:

➤ Many terrific startup and grown-up businesses define marketing as a communications function, and activate marketing efforts too late and too superficially to realize impact.

➤ How marketing is defined influences the talent hired—the balance between strategist and tactician, end user versus distribution expert, and how these people integrate with the rest of the organization.

➤ Calculating marketing ROI has always been art and science. Today, the magnitude of data, and processing capability, lead some to assume that absolute precision is possible and necessary. But reality is that added complexity won't add value to the good enough answers that work for starters.

➤ Public relations can play a role—if you have a newsworthy story. The press defines how newsworthy the story is. Don't expect to control the press. PR is not free marketing.

➤ Influencers have mattered long before any of us could spell d-i-g-i-t-a-l. Lasting influencer support on social media or elsewhere is earned by creating and delivering value.

What marketplace actions stimulate trial and sales?

To navigate the choices and decisions toward a great marketing plan:

➤ **Keep as guideposts** the work you have done on purpose, market insights, user and buyer profiles and needs, and business model assumptions. Put a Post-it on your computer, a reminder on your phone screen. Give yourself the twenty-first-century equivalent of the string around your finger to avoid being dazzled and distracted by short-lived shiny objects that look like silver bullet solutions.

➤ **Get the right creative and media partners.** If this means an agency, avoid getting caught up in hiring the name over the door. Assess the team assigned to you on a daily basis, the culture fit, and whether there is strong belief in your vision. The cool work done for some other brand is unimportant.

➤ **Don't overbuild marketing infrastructure.** Marketing automation and analytics software is useful, but start with the basics to understand what you can really use. Thousands of mar-tech solutions are out there. Minimize complexity. Tools don't by themselves solve problems. Conduct thorough diligence to understand how tools work, how they affect your business model drivers, and what is required for you to take advantage of new capabilities.

Why is behavioral segmentation critical?

Segmentation is so much more than a conceptual way to organize data for media buying or content delivery. Segmentation is a capability that sets up a business to deliver on customer expectations. Segmentation establishes the basis for viable economics, including market size, costs to create offerings, and how to attract and engage customers, fulfill orders, and manage and service relationships.

Demographic, psychographic, media consumption, and other traditional segmentation model variables are useful, but not sufficient to create productive segments. Buyer behavior and preferences for your offering turn out to weigh heavily on marketing returns.

Say your concept requires a level of income or assets, or profession, or living arrangement to be relevant or accessible. Makes sense to knock out people who don't have the ability or need to be served by you.

Now go further, and define the predominant ways people seek information and then interact, buy, and transact. While buying lots of third-party data is possible, far greater value will come from investing in understanding how users and buyers engage with your product, service, or experience. So dig into even the small volume of data your pre-launch testing has produced to structure the launch plan. Then see how other sources can be additive.

What are the thought processes, the action steps, the advice sought by a potential user or buyer—planning a vacation, doing home renovations, shopping for Christmas gifts, purchasing software? Patterns of behavior will suggest segments, and inform prioritization and how to use resources.

Behavior-based segmentation allows marketers to connect with customers where they already are, doing what they already do. It avoids waste. Applying even the basic principles increases returns on marketing investment, so will earn greater investor support.

Proceed at your peril without thoughtful segment analytics and selection. Know what segment members' lives are about, how the brand fits in, and how customer behaviors and business levers, offering, and experience connect to the launch marketing plan.

How do user and buyer segments work in an intermediated business?

Within the life insurance sector, segments were historically defined by agents' own networks, largely made up of friends and family. Digital channels provide opportunity to reach even further. This is an aspirational yet potentially threatening innovation for a business model built on commissioning agents to push complex products.

A global insurance carrier took the path toward establishing ground-breaking and actionable segmentation plans:

➤ Using qualitative insight discovery findings, the business defined eight segments along three dimensions: life event "triggers," discrete channel behaviors and preferences, and client decision-making styles.

➤ Quantitative analysis confirmed the eight segments.

➤ Qualitative findings informed maps of user and buyer journeys within each segment, beginning with how awareness of unmet needs surfaced, how options were explored, shopping, influencers, decision-making, purchase, and payment.

➤ Last, the potential of each segment was projected, including the number of policy buyers, and the insurance coverage likely to be purchased. These estimates drove resource allocation, and pushed four segments higher as investment priorities.

➤ Client database records were tagged with segment identifiers, enabling sales and marketing program targeting of media and message as a first step.

All of this effort resulted in an expanded, organized, and actionable view of market segments, and recommendations for marketing, product development, user experience, and technology capabilities linked to business model and strategy goals. The segmentation findings also challenged long-held beliefs inhibiting growth. They triggered change management to increase internal buy-in.

Introducing segmentation opened the possibility for a tradition-bound business to move beyond techniques that were producing diminishing returns.

Which metrics are right for launch?

Align launch metrics to the strategy. Metrics should codify the promises made to executives and investors, and link strategy to reality. Factors to create metrics:

➤ Work backward from the goals.

➤ Measure the *drivers*—the user and buyer behaviors that move the business model. Of course the outcomes are where the buck stops, but drivers are where outcomes are influenced and where a team has leverage to create results.

➤ Pay attention to leading indicators allowing you to be proactive.

➤ Do your best to ensure that results will be available to allow you to take action based on what is happening, e.g., with media and other marketing elements.

Let's say the need is for a segment beachhead. Figure out the threshold for a starting presence. Then, set goals based on attributes such as:

➤ Who and how many people are buying?

➤ Where are they buying?

➤ What is the customer's path to discovery, trial, and purchase?

➤ What feedback can you discern—both observed and inferred?

➤ Are there expected patterns of buyer behavior, or surprises?

Combining the right array of data points provides a picture of what is happening and reveals where the leverage is for next steps.

The more innovative the offering the less likely rearview mirror data helps. Setting metrics or targets based on a legacy product is a mistake. Think about it, if you are driving down an unfamiliar road, how much time do you spend looking backward?

Metrics are possible to ground even disruptive innovation. Metrics do not always fit onto spreadsheets, calculated with lengthy algorithms. Rigor is relative. Metrics can be derived from qualitative insight. For example, starting metrics might gauge emotional reaction intensity, by observing people as they pick up your product from an end aisle display. You can measure how long users stay within your digital experience and where they linger to explore—or where you lose them. Apply a high, medium, low scale—or red, yellow, green—to start. Be reasonable. Don't impose precision where it makes no sense.

Five summary points to remember when choosing metrics:

1. Whether metrics matter depends upon their contribution to improved decisions. Ask, "So what?"

2. Metrics evolve. Put a few concrete stakes in the ground, and increase precision as launch efforts continue.

3. Within grown-up companies there is a bad habit of assessing innovations with pre-digital metrics of scale businesses. If this sounds familiar, break the habit.

4. Recognize that sometimes common sense plays a bigger role to select useful launch metrics than advanced statistical techniques.

5. Translate what the metrics say into rapid improvements.

Advice from a master launcher: What to do and how to do it

Geoff Chellis, president of Expedia Consulting Group, has launched over seventy pharmaceutical and financial services products, at global corporations and startups. He gets called upon for the toughest launches. His common sense approach is packed with pointers to make the complex manageable.

I call Geoff the "master launcher" not only because of the number of launches he has facilitated, but because he has done so in two highly complex sectors. His recommendations for results:

➤ **Define what "good" looks like.** Begin by identifying the key functions necessary for a launch. Then recruit internal leaders and lead a kickoff meeting to establish a common vision for launch success.

➤ **Focus on what matters most.** Set clear expectations on the high-priority deliverables for launch. Focus attention on critical issues and strategic decisions the team needs resolved to execute their plans. Geoff advises, "Once the team has bought into the big ticket items and dependencies, get out of their way to pull the tactics off."[8]

➤ **Keep your options open.** Insist that the team test multiple paths to launch and monitor progress diligently to select the best approach as insights emerge. "The optimal approach is rarely identified at the start," Geoff notes. "The answer comes from pursuing several options, then doubling up efforts where you get traction and cutting your losses quickly on non-starters."

➤ **Plan for success.** Define best case, base case, and worst case outcomes, particularly for timing, but set the timetable to hit the earliest possible launch date. Everyone is accountable to that date. Setbacks are inevitable but it is far easier to shift back in time than scramble for positive surprises when everything goes right. And for sure, management or investors will quickly embrace any newfound upside faster than a team can pick up the pace. Geoff says, "For a new drug racing the patent clock, timing changes are material. Slippage can be a career ender."

➤ **Anticipate uncertainty.** Meet frequently to pressure check plans and identify places where the launch may break down, so you anticipate problems and define contingencies before they disrupt your plans. A word of caution, adds Geoff, "Midcourse corrections are to be encouraged provided they are explicitly stated. Otherwise people may be solving their own problem and unknowingly creating problems for other functions."

➤ **Launch strong.** Fast followers can find ways to follow right behind a competitor's launch. Geoff says, "Your success or failure depends upon how successful you are out of the gate. Hit a strong trajectory." Stumbles allow openings for others to capitalize on your mistakes.

➤ **Keep it simple.** Do not pile on to the launch or accept complexity without upside. Avoid the unnecessary to ensure clarity of focus and speed to market. "It's easy to get bogged down in minutiae. Keep the focus on each function's critical deliverables so the launch stays on track," says Geoff. He adds, "Better to follow with successive waves of launch initiatives that build on your launch and keep your competitors guessing."

➤ **Promote constructive behavior.** It is up to the leader to create a safe environment to take chances and accept setbacks, while not letting anyone off the hook. Geoff says, "Not a month goes by that I don't have someone in tears. Launches are stressful. I tell them, 'we are good people challenged to do the impossible.' " Live the values, stick to purpose, and keep attention on the strategic decisions that matter most.

THE THREE Cs OF LAUNCH

Capabilities:

Project management: To conquer complexity, keep it simple

The larger and more complex the project, the more helpful a simple approach to project management is. This means one that:

1. Keeps the team together by letting everyone know what is going on,

2. Is easy to keep current and understand, and

3. Lets each team member decide how to manage their detailed plan and deliverables.

The Tools:

1. **Implement weekly project summaries.** Insist on back-of-the-envelope project summaries from each function that show key deliverables, steps, and timing in two pages or less. Bring

the team together for a weekly ninety-minute launch readiness review. This meeting is about cross-team dependencies that may not be top-of-mind the rest of the week. The focus should be on "big ticket" items, key dependencies, and areas prone to bottlenecks.

Make it comfortable to flag issues without finger-pointing, since there is little chance everything is on track if the team is held to the best-case outcome.

Why project summaries work. Brevity ensures the team sees the big picture, key dependencies, and critical paths at a glance. Consistency of reporting promotes cross-team under-standing, reduces the burden to keep them current, and frees each individual team to choose the tools and process that work best for them to manage the underlying details.

2. Biweekly executive/investor update. A three-section pres-entation style summary, length equivalent to one page per topic. The brevity of all communications demands thought clarity, and results in high-impact communication. The con-tent:

- **Slide 1:** Accomplishments of the past two weeks, and milestones that are coming up in the next two weeks
- **Slide 2:** An executive view of major work streams in "swim lanes," making important dates and integration points easy to see
- **Slide 3:** A short list of critical items that should be on the team's and executives' radar, for discussion and resolution

Why this update works: Executives and investors with short attention spans and limited time want to know whether launch is on track, how risks are being managed, and where the team could use help.

#1: Project leads use a common project summary tool

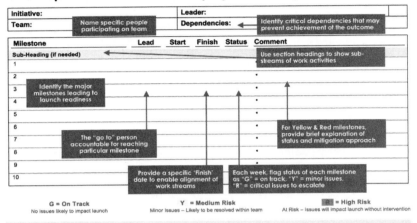

#2: Key items summarized in one-pager for team reviews

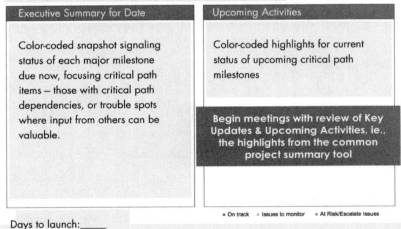

#3: A high level timeline informs leadership

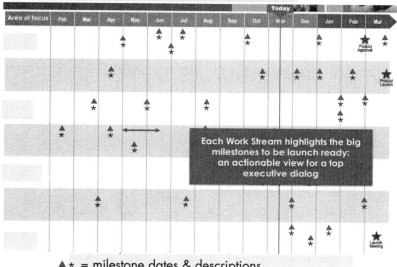

Today

Area of focus	Feb	Mar	Apr	May	Jun	Jul	Aug	Sep	Oct	Nov	Dec	Jan	Feb	Mar

Each Work Stream highlights the big milestones to be launch ready: an actionable view for a top executive dialog

Product Approval

Product Launch

Launch Meeting

▲★ = milestone dates & descriptions

#4: Focus on critical areas and strategic decisions

Area of Focus	Concern / Decision Required	Owner	Due	Status of Discussions	Decision Steps & Timing

Critical Strategic Issues That Cut Across Teams Are Vigilantly Pursued and Monitored

• On track • Issues to monitor • At Risk/Escalate Issues

The who/what/what strategic communications brief

An agency partner once said to me, "Clients get the work that they deserve." To get great work, creative and media talent are more effective when clearly briefed on the assignment. This applies to internal and agency talent.

There are many briefing formats. A personal favorite is the "who/what/what."

No matter the format you end up using, any brief should be based on the insights gathered through discovery. A brief is based on market insight, not made up. And, a brief must be written down.

Aside from its simplicity, what is great about the who/what/what format is that the answers to the three prompts not only inform the launch and future marketing assignments. The approach works for any communication, from a quick chat to an email to a major speech or presentation. When the communications are essential, answer the who/what/what questions before opening your mouth or crafting the written message.

The who/what/what brief has just three sections: **Who is the audience?** This section describes demographics, attitudes, behaviors, beliefs, preferences, and problems of each primary segment. It is not meant to be a data compilation. Synthesize into personae what you know from market insights about the target audiences. One way to know whether your synthesis is useful: If you ran into a member of your target segment on the street, would you immediately recognize them, and be able to strike up an engaging conversation?

> 1. **What does the audience believe today?** Relative to the problem your product solves, write a brief narrative, in the voice of the segment, describing feelings, experiences, wishes,

needs, hopes, wants. What does resolution of the problem look and feel like from the target segment's perspective?

2. What do you want the audience to believe after experiencing your offer and brand? How do you want to influence? The narrative in this section goes well beyond, "I will buy the product." How, in the target segment's words, are you causing them to feel, respond, and behave as a result of your messaging, product, and experience?

The who/what/what briefing

Who is the target audience? Demographics, attitudes, behaviors, beliefs, problems of each key segment. Would you know your audience if you met up with them?
What do they believe currently about the problem you are solving? I.e., what are the feelings, experiences, wishes, needs, hopes and wants of target segments relative to the problem you are solving?
What would you like the audience to believe after experiencing your brand? I.e., how is your target audience feeling, responding and behaving as a result of your messaging, product, and experience?

Connections:

What agency partner connections are needed to establish awareness, contribute to developing brand positioning, and deliver revenue goals? To be effective, agencies need to know what your needs are—your strategy, business objectives, timeframes. They need transparency in a daily working relationship. They are not magicians; like everyone contributing to launch, they need direction, a setup for success, and defined outcomes.

The focus on marketing will intensify. Start with a clear assignment, defining the skills required, and how you plan to work together. Do a clean sheet assessment of what marketing capabilities are needed. Then decide what role an agency or other partner will play versus internal marketing talent.

➤ What skills and fit are necessary to deliver the strategy?

➤ Where is the best talent? Can you attract them?

➤ Do you have ongoing or point-in-time needs?

➤ What do budgets allow? Is fixed or variable preferable at this point?

➤ Do you have the leadership and marketing skills to manage agency partners?

If the decision is to include an agency, getting to a short list and then making the final choice has become more complicated by the disruption of the agency sector itself. Is marketing a creative, analytics, communications, experience, or technology function? It is all of these and more. To meet this expanding definition, agency services are becoming more diverse. Offerings have become fragmented. The big agency holding companies claim to offer the total solution via the smaller shops they acquire. Look for evidence of real coordination if that is the pitch you are hearing. Specialized skills of small, independent agencies will require coordination—and demand your team's time, talent, and attention.

Still, success depends upon the basics: tying user and buyer insights to a purpose-based positioning and marketing plan that resonate to target audiences and drive the business model.

Following is a framework to sort out marketing capabilities helpful for launch. Some may belong within the team and others can be led or supported by partners. A combination of internal and external capabilities is likely. Count on extra effort to brief, manage, and establish accountability for external partner results. Hiring an agency does not mean over-the-fence outsourcing. Great agency work comes from a collaborative, open relationship where roles are clear, and expertise is in place and respected. Give focused assignments driven by user, buyer, and broader market insights.

Assembling Marketing Capabilities for Launch

THE CAPABILITY	WHAT DOES THE CAPABILITY ENABLE?
Defining the marketing strategy	Synthesizes the go-to-market elements of the strategy, e.g., • Brand strategy • Customer segment(s) • Product and experience benefits, features • Success metrics (e.g., leads, activation, engagement, retention, loyalty) • Budget and milestones
Understanding audiences and their context, motivations, values, and needs	Leads insights and analytics to understand users and buyers • Insights about segments, intermediaries, influencers • Use of data and insight to implement and create value • Market, competitive context
Advancing and evolving the value proposition	Brings forward new concepts to stay ahead of trends • Collaborates on prototype development and testing for what's next • Success metrics (e.g., leads, activation, engagement, retention, loyalty) • Budget and milestones
Creating the brand promise	Translates purpose into actionable brand deliverables • Brand positioning • Brand architecture • Tactics, e.g., experience, packaging, customer service messaging, etc.
Optimizing channels	Determines how to deploy resources across channels based on customer behavior and business goals • Social media, digital channels, devices, influencers • Media mix—physical, virtual, mobile • Multichannel—linkage to how people discover, shop, and buy.
Executing the marketing plan	Implementing • Managing the agency, external partners • Media buying • Marketing collateral—sales materials • Sponsorships, events, PR
Measuring and learning	Designing and implementing methods to measure results and anticipate what's next • Brand and customer satisfaction • Return on marketing investment (ROMI); spend optimization • Real time feedback loops

Culture:

Cultural attributes for successful launch include:

➤ **Moving with speed and urgency** without diminishing the brand purpose and promise

➤ **Showing obsessive user focus** through execution challenges

➤ **Creative problem solving** as a habit

➤ **Decisive**, knowing that 70 percent of the information is enough, and too much information is harmful

➤ **Adaptable** in real time

➤ **Optimistic** especially under the pressure of daily ambiguity

➤ **Open and transparent**, seeing net upside to sharing problems

➤ **Outcome oriented**, always focused on achieving results

➤ **Accountable**, proactively acknowledging when it is time to course correct

➤ **Maintaining a fear-free environment** where everyone speaks up

➤ **Remembering to celebrate** the big and small wins

Chapter summary

➤ Launch is when the team delivers the brand promise to market, and sets the trajectory to deliver business model expectations.

➤ Having paused (however quickly) for the green-light moment, launch capabilities are forming or in place. Otherwise, pause and confirm readiness.

➤ As focus on driving sales intensifies, keep sight of the passion, purpose, and market insights that led to this point. Convenient short-term tradeoffs water down great solutions and reduce chances of passing the 10x test.

➤ A good launch is more likely when there are common sense metrics, individuals take accountability for outcomes, and problems are surfaced before they happen.

➤ Seek out launch lessons from other sectors and company types. Extreme launches, such as those happening in pharmaceuticals and financial services, include valuable insight for any sector and company stage.

➤ Marketing planning, talent, and agency roles are defining decisions for launch success. Take advantage of proven rules of thumb, methods, and tools to onboard the best creative, media, and marketing technology and analytics talent to establish a strong revenue trajectory.

CHAPTER 8:
Testing and Experimenting

Coming up through the ranks at two payments giants, I took for granted the extent to which testing and experimenting were baked into everything we did. Even before imagining the possibilities of digital and mobile, payments companies worked with big data, analytics, and technology to experiment with communications, channel, products, personalization, and promotional strategies.

Testing was how we improved operations—customer selection, line of credit calculations, offer targeting, and repayment risk. We experimented to figure out ways to meet business model requirements under given conditions. We saw testing as a huge positive, the fastest and most cost-effective way to get ahead of the market, understand revenue and expense levers, anticipate and avoid risk, and create value and growth. The channels up until the mid-nineties just happened to be mail and phone.

So my eyes were opened when I left the sector and had two aha's:

➤ Most companies are not realizing the unique advantages of testing and experimenting, and

➤ Testing and experimenting works best in a culture that values learning about what is not working as much as confirming what is working.

For change makers, the stakes are too high to rely on guesswork. Seat-of-the-pants may have been necessary in the past, but today's complexity, competition, and demands to achieve scale all require more. There is too much information, too many choices and decisions, and too little time. Expectations are high, while the effects of innovation investments can be difficult to discern.

Strong testing and experimenting come from mindset, capabilities, investment, and commitment. The starter elements may already be within reach, even inside your head.

Direct-to-consumer and transaction-based business models, such as that of credit cards businesses, have long-valued data sciences capabilities. These companies have proven that testing and experimenting effectiveness depends upon:

➤ **Knowing the business priority.** What is the goal? Can you decompose the goal into distinct variables?

➤ **Creating a strategy-driven learning agenda.** What questions do you want to answer? What are the hypotheses that link to priorities?

➤ **Structuring tests and experiments.** Most organizations miss on population selection. Poor choices bury cross-effects that yield false reads.

➤ **Following through on post-test analysis.** Tests yield more insight than anticipated, but most organizations restrict themselves to simple analysis and don't pursue insights to potential windfalls.

➤ **Keeping an inventory of testing.** Results of experiments are goldmines. You can keep digging, but that requires maintaining a trail of what has been tested before.

Testing and experimenting is constant for any business creating value and growth.

More is required than statistics, data clouds, and number-crunching tools. This chapter is devoted to setting out testing and experimenting requirements. The principles fit scale efforts of all sizes, shapes, and stages.

Don't be thrown off course by the jargon surrounding artificial intelligence, big data, machine learning, and whatever else is coming next. There is plenty of confusion. The marketplace for automation offerings is large and fragmented.

The good news is that there are lots of examples from which to borrow. Technology is accessible. Data is abundant. Storage is cheap.

Assumptions about testing and experimenting:

➤ There is no excuse not to test, experiment, and apply learning;

➤ Testing and experimenting capabilities create a competitive wedge;

➤ Testing and experimenting require skills, knowledge integration, infrastructure, and a learning culture;

➤ New offers are pushed to us all whenever we turn on our devices. The pace of change is constant. Most offers are incremental.

Testing and experimenting keep startup and grown-up businesses on pace. Even better, they point to marketplace discontinuities leading to innovation.

Surprise: Marketers have conducted A/B tests for a long time

The first known instances of direct mail trace back to 1000 BC.[1] Modern-day testing tactics have origins at least back to the early 1960s, when agency executive Lester Wunderman gets credit for coining the term "direct marketing."[2] Testing was structured against control groups. On the edges of direct mail and telemarketing programs, test cells were created allowing for tight measurement of changes to offer, pricing, communications, targeting, and channel. Results were read—maybe beginning within days of deploying, but possibly weeks or even months later—and winners adopted.

Such testing measured and valued execution tactics to decide investments in programs whose pre-digital timeframes were long and whose costs were high. The goals were to find incremental improvements, validate hypotheses, and justify new campaign strategies. Teams debated details, such as the precise level of statistical significance to apply to each test for results to be accepted as empirically sound. Precision was achievable.

Measurement and optimization are quite different from experimentation pursued to shape and scale innovation. Traditional techniques still matter, especially in scale businesses with mature methods to acquire and retain customers. But the speed at which feedback can be obtained with an explosion of variables has disrupted the slow and steady structures of the past. Now it is essential to find ways to pick up bits of precision as needed in shorter, faster cycles. Machine learning is creating an entirely new paradigm—one where testing is built into ongoing self-learning campaigns.

Traditional testing depended upon market opportunities holding still. Today nothing holds still. But there are still principles and patterns, some of which have been proven through decades. So, even when there is no fixed template, rigor is achievable.

Testing and experimenting: "Just the way we work"

Startup Pypestream's Smart Messaging Platform uses artificial intelligence and chat bots to connect businesses to their customers. Chief customer officer Donna Peeples brings dual perspective on the value of testing and experimenting, having also served as an executive at major corporations including AIG. She says, "The difference I've seen is that in the corporate world testing is formalized and structured. In startup land, we don't even call testing out as a separate activity. It is just the way we work. It's very iterative and very fluid. There is no line of demarcation between testing, experimenting, and everything else."[3]

Integrating testing and experimenting into how a team operates takes a systematic, flexible approach to extracting insights from many forms of data—and then taking action. It's not about data for the sake of data, or tools for the sake of having the latest number-crunching capability, or data storage for the sake of volume. You may be starting with a clean sheet. You may be jury-rigging your first learning platform, or trying to get out from under the constraints of a rigid, overly complicated one. There are common themes.

Eric Sandosham, cofounder of Singapore-based Red & White Consulting Partners, agrees. He says, "Startups are naturally predisposed to testing and experimenting simply because they have so little historic data to draw upon, and no existing business to defend. These factors make them extremely agile. They can evaluate insights with no stake in the past so they are better able to detect emerging opportunities."[4]

What are you trying to figure out?

Decide which of the three types of insight apply to your priorities:

➤ **Hindsight, or descriptive results explaining what happened.** Are results up, down, or sideways? What customer behaviors occur in different channels, or as a result of a marketing program? Did you even know that competition has begun to eat your lunch? Can shining a light on the issue by testing be the wake-up call your organization needs?

➤ **Insight, or diagnostic results, explaining why something happened.** Has pricing affected sales? Has a change someplace between the product team and point of purchase caused a problem that must be pinned down? Diagnostic results uncover execution improvements, building upon what is known from past performance data.

➤ **Foresight, or progressive insights, about how to make something happen.** Are you trying to find the next problem to solve to change market position? Can applying the model of scientific exploration reveal the next innovation? Foresight takes listening, dot-connecting, and then interpreting feedback—multiple sources, through multiple cycles of analysis, with reasonable judgment playing an interpretation role.

Three critical thinking guideposts

No matter the path, consider scribbling these guideposts on sticky notes tacked up in your workspace:

1. Define the questions leading to decisions and action, linked to strategic priorities.

2. Know the business-model operating levers—user behavior, processes, policies, and regulation. All drive financials.

3. Have the execution capability to apply models, including each test result. If not, what is the point of the test?

Ten testing and experimenting pitfalls

1. Confusing learning priorities and methodology. Mismatching hindsight, insight, and foresight goals with test approach has penalties. An A/B test is productive to determine relative impact of alternative pricing, offers, messages, or channels. If head-to-head testing is not feasible, pre- and post-testing can work. But neither is relevant if the goal is to foresee performance of an unprecedented idea, where metrics may not even be quantifiable at the outset.

2. Failing to stay connected to start and end points. Customer insights, business model, goals, priorities, and strategy are always linchpins to value and growth. They frame testing and experimenting priorities, too.

3. Pursuing flawed testing paths. A proposed test becomes so complicated it cannot be implemented. A team defines legitimate test questions. As design is sketched out, more permutations of segments and offers are added. The team strays from priorities.

4. Becoming overwhelmed by data. Everything seems knowable. The most valuable data—substantially more valuable than third party overlays—will be data about your customers' engagement with you. Apply art and science to sort "need to know," "nice to know," and "really no need to know" data.

5. Coming at the world technology first. Technology is an enabler. By itself even the slickest analytics tool can add complexity and expense that subtracts value. Match tools to the task and the talent.

6. Producing results that are not actionable. Tests so clean that they are isolated from the realities of processes, policies, and regulations take time and effort with no practical impact.

7. Over-devotion to a method. Agile methodology is a force for speed, focusing teams on what's good enough. Teams benefit from standardizing cycles—implement, read, react, repeat. But solving for time to the point of inflexibility blocks experiments that only come with time and messiness.

8. Expecting the test to tell you what to do. Testing produces insights and raises additional questions. Think critically to decide which results to act upon and which new questions are worth pursuing.

9. Rejecting findings at odds with the status quo. A test or experiment is well designed and executed. The findings fly in the face of orthodoxies. Conflict ensues. Politics takes over. Status quo is maintained. Opportunities are missed. This scene is unfortunately familiar when the data suggest a future that causes discomfort among people satisfied with the current state, or fearful of change.

10. Not establishing and leveraging an inventory of testing. An inventory affords opportunity to gain speed, connect dots, and provide a knowledge base of discoveries waiting for the right timing to put them to work.

Moving to action through small, manageable steps

How can you make a habit of sensing where there is useful data, analyzing, synthesizing, assessing, and then applying findings quickly? For the answer I sought input from Marcia Tal. Marcia advises executives on advancing innovative data science and technology-based solutions. For much of her career, Marcia was busy inventing, shaping, and leading Citi Decision Management, a powerhouse global function.

A rocket scientist by training, Marcia has a way of patiently breaking down multilayered problems into useful pieces. She defines problem statements to generate tests and experiments. Outputs provide solutions to complex problems by identifying and addressing the component levers. Outputs build momentum for change by creating fact bases that wear down even the toughest resistors and surface unexpected opportunity.

Marcia advises focusing first on internal data sources. She says, "Internal data will always be the most valuable. Other sources won't replace proprietary data—they can complement it."[5]

Not collecting or maintaining a strong customer database? Make it a priority to figure out how to address this gap.

Next, know how the business operates to construct, execute, and interpret tests. Especially important is to understand how customers make decisions that define behavior with the brand.

Marcia shares a wonderful family anecdote highlighting the impact of paying attention to data and seeing insights through to action:

> For decades around the 1950s, my uncle Norman owned a store—Norman's Everybody Store—in Tulsa, Oklahoma. He would ask everybody who came through the door the same question: "What do you need?" That was his way of gathering data. He could sell anything, and he did, from cowboy boots to hats to women's pajamas to lingerie to men's underwear. And he applied a very important insight to his location— always next to a bar. What data drove the insight? He knew that people went to the bar after they got paid. So he knew when they had cash, and he wanted to be second in line, after the bartender, to get some of it.

Norman understood his business-model levers. He gathered and applied data about how customer behavior drove sales. He aligned his location strategy to take advantage of a findable and measurable business driver.

At Norman's Everybody Store, learning from data was as much a part of how things worked as it is today at Pypestream.

Sure, understanding and acting upon customer data back in Norman's day may look primitive from the perspective of our Amazon world. But what Norman lacked in technology was more than offset by mindset and translation of insights into decisions.

Reminder: don't let vast data and new technologies take you away from the basics of knowing the operating levers within the business model, including understanding customer behavior. No amount of cool technology or data will make up for lack of attention to these essentials.

Focus on the gaps when designing tests

"You will get lost if you don't keep going back to the question, 'What am I trying to do?'" says Angela Curry, former managing director, Global Analytics & Insights at Citi. "Understand the goals. Where do you need insight? Build tests from there."[6]

An easy way to gauge a well-defined goal is to fill in the blank in this sentence: "We will be successful in our venture if _____ happens."

Is success attracting a certain number of users? Getting to a particular level of engagement or a market share goal or a sales volume target? The way you complete the sentence signals the data-driven learning priorities.

Gaps occur because too many teams construct tests without first thinking about what success means. They get caught in the data weeds and don't build momentum. What is the objective? In post-MVP start-ups through mature businesses, success means hitting the annual plan. A business unit's plan numbers may be high level, but they also frame expectations. Every test design should ultimately contribute to achieving the plan.

Your plan may not be as formalized as that of a business unit inside a global, publicly traded company, but whatever plan you have developed defines a horizon line. That horizon line is the direction for test efforts.

Plan

Tackle feasibility questions by considering each business-model lever that might impact the test. Figure out which ones do, and address the consequences. Engaged stakeholders are a big help. You may know your product really well, or be closely familiar with how channels work. Odds are you don't know all of the operating details. So include people who do. Topics for these conversations:

➤ Will tests be readable, with outputs the team can understand and use to impact performance? What measures is the test designed to generate?

➤ What are the requirements and work effort to implement the test? Have you defined phase one, understanding that this is likely the first of many cycles?

➤ Do regulations affect processes? Do policies define decision rules affecting test execution? Such impacts can come between customer response and the end result.

➤ Who are the stakeholders, both to run the test and support findings? Are stakeholders on board to the test design, metrics, assumptions and limitations, implementation plan, success standards, and next steps?

➤ Are external stakeholders interested in the test, e.g., regulators or consumer advocates? Are their needs being addressed?

➤ Are partners required to implement testing, and execute changes based on findings?

Design experiments yielding metrics that close gaps between performance and goals. Do you want to acquire more customers, and if so, at what cost? Is the goal to expand margins, and if so, by how much? Is your leverage in pricing, distribution, communications, positioning, or product configuration? Do you anticipate new risks, and if so, how can a test validate or disprove mitigation strategies?

What measurement precision is reasonable and necessary? In a mature space with back history, expect greater precision. But if there is less precedent, get comfortable with directional outputs in the early testing of hypotheses. Be ready to build on each new insight to refine, and then refine some more. Accept that attribution of impact across many variables may be a work-in-progress. You may not even realize what all the variables are until after several test cycles.

By laying out the range of priority test questions before diving into the details, it becomes possible to realize the advantages of an integrated plan and avoid the inefficiencies and errors caused by fragmented testing. This discipline also mitigates hindsight bias risk. When people look at results and say, "We already knew that," the value of testing is diminished. Validation that doesn't become over-testing—an excuse to avoid a decision—can be useful. Just be sensitive to motivations and unintended consequences.

Go for impact by striking the balance between testing scope, complexity, and speed. Prioritize the "need to knows." Push back on "let's add this" temptations.

A pragmatic way to validate the metrics: create a prototype of the results dashboard before launching any tests. Then ask, "What will we do with these results? Where are the answers to the questions we must answer now?" If the answers to these questions are clear, the metrics are on track. If you are spinning in circles coming up with the answers, take action to add missing pieces or edit out extraneous, low priority data.

Assemble the right mix of people for testing and experimenting success

Pre-digital era testing used internal data sets, complemented by a few external overlays. Now, data is accessible from multiple sources, in structured and unstructured formats, in real time. The multichannel customer experience, with its many dimensions, affects sales, returns, repurchase and referrals, out-of-stock product, and ratings and reviews. This complexity intensifies the benefits of a cross-functional skillset— creativity, critical thinking, analytical, technical, operational—whatever perspectives apply to the business-model levers in the daily activities of running the business.

As with any tough problem, diversity of thought and experience opens the pathways to better, faster solutions.

Even if one person is accountable for all aspects of testing, two persona types make testing and experimenting work better:

The planner: Someone who is able to anticipate whether, what, and when testing will be influenced by the operations, processes, or policies of a business. They account for these realities in test design and planning. In a complex business, it's impossible to anticipate all connections and how they interact without engaging people who know the plumbing and the wiring. The planner identifies and integrates multiple perspectives. They connect the dots between test design and implementation. They are a strategic jack-of-all-trades.

The implementer: This person has hands-on knowledge of analytics tools and methods. Perhaps they are a mathematician or technologist. Such backgrounds provide foundational implementer skill sets. Data is vast and varied, sources expand, and tools change. So what they know today may be obsolete in a few quarters. That is why the implementer who shines is skilled in how to look for information, read and write code to set up tests, and adapt to new techniques.

The planner and the implementer are both motivated to learn. Both are collaborators: if they are not one and the same person, they need each other.

Both benefit from a sustained ability to figure things out on the fly. What is going through their heads is this: "I don't necessarily need to know everything, but I can figure things out or tap into others for help."

The infrastructure and tools for testing and experimenting success

Infrastructure matters. If basics are not in place, pulling off a test plan will be challenging. Assemble the components—data sources, campaign management, analytics software, how data is captured, and how it links to partner systems. Ask:

➤ What must be automated?

➤ Where is the investment to automate not yet justified?

➤ Do you know enough to choose the right tools?

➤ Is it better to seek providers with functional or sector expertise?

Just as in test design, go back to the problem statement, strategy, and implementation details to make automation decisions.

Say the focus is to test content. Which content is worth testing? If you are delivering content across channels, is the capability in place to pull the channel messaging together—or will silos limit what can be tested, read, and delivered? If the vision is to achieve the holy grail of one-to-one personalization, how do you create content, subject lines, offers for individuals, and execute dynamically?

Or say the customer journey spans digital and physical channels. Where along the path from creating awareness, to investigating options, to buying and then post-purchasing experiences is value created? Is customer behavior interpretable across channels, or are channel data disconnected? What is the plan to justify or overcome limitations?

Finally, getting full value from infrastructure is more than a function of picking and implementing the right tools. An example of a challenge: A company's corporate email platform was different than that used by the sales force. There was no automated way to assemble all of the interactions with a customer across both platforms. Focus was placed on coordinating these channels to align infrastructure with the organization's goal of improving sales and engagement. The business model drivers, power and authority, and politics all came into play to make this happen.

Even if your own skills are cutting edge and the team is dogged, infrastructure predating current data integration and flexibility demands can disable well-conceived testing goals.

Licensing a tool to address a capability gap is a widely used approach. Software providers help set up tests and produce results for digital and mobile testing in real time. Is budget tight? Maybe the latest version of a tool is not necessary. Perhaps it would be smarter to go the do-it-yourself route for a few iterations, confirm you are on the right path, and then choose a solution. Free tools, especially in the early days of figuring out your requirements, may be all you need.

What is the condition of your database? For starters:

> Are records in one dataset, or in different parts of the infrastructure? Is data in organizational silos, off-limits to others because of decision rights, legal vehicle structure, or regulation?

➤ Is the database searchable? Can records be easily tagged, e.g., with segment indicators?

➤ Can imports and exports be done readily?

➤ What about data overlays from third-party providers?

➤ Is history maintained for contacts, service inquiries, responses to offers, and channel usage?

➤ What compliance rules govern use of the database?

➤ Are website and mobile applications set up for testing flexibility?

➤ Is whatever digital analytics package in use correctly implemented and robust enough to support priorities?

Partnering for testing and experimenting success

When to partner is a function of answers to questions including:

➤ Will a partner bring capability you don't have?

➤ Do potential partners have better talent? Many demands are baked in to the profile of the planner and implementer. Can you attract the best, or should you tap into freelance, consulting, or agency resources?

➤ Do you have budget to hire and build internally, or is a variable cost approach more pragmatic?

➤ Don't be dazzled by the partner's reputation based on PR, or the sign over the door. Who is going to work on your business, the A Team or the B Team? Does the partner team share your passion and sense of purpose?

Use common sense to invest for impact

Each test is an investment. Don't avoid testing to protect every last short-term dollar of revenue, but don't harm the business for the sake of a test, either. Some tests will pay out quickly and some will lead to the next set of tests.

A senior marketing executive at a direct-to-consumer brand serving over thirty million users shared a story about testing to quantify the impact of specific channels on new accounts. The company's marketing activities bring together search, site, mobile advertising, direct mail, and telemarketing in integrated campaigns.

One of the proposals floated was to measure the contribution of search by turning it off for three months.

CMOs are eager to understand how to attribute marketing spend to each channel. But common sense says that the practical consequences of shutting down a channel as important as search, even if such a tactic could yield a precise answer, likely outweigh benefits.

The CMO or CFO or business unit head may resist carving out even a small testing population. Tests may not produce immediate improvements. Such pushback is shortsighted, but exists in organizations that do not yet fully embrace a testing and experimenting mindset.

Tackle reality

Rarely until teams get into the thick of implementation and executing on findings are the operational requirements for testing and experimenting understood and appreciated.

Be eyes-wide-open:

➤ Testing is an ongoing commitment, not a one-time event.

➤ Infrastructure gaps raise obstacles at big and small, young and old companies. Diagnose what is possible now, what must change, and how to close infrastructure gaps.

➤ Testing and experimenting take investment in people, tools, and data infrastructure. There is a cost to every test: for each test some proven action is not being taken. The potential for return exceeding the cost has to be there, at least as a hypothesis.

Bring people along. Getting test results to take hold starts with science and lands squarely with people and their emotions. Learning from tests drives improvement. Learning is not a vehicle for spotlighting failure or mistakes.

Back in Chapter 5, the tools of storytelling were presented in the context of selling the business model to investors. Now, consider how to relate the story that emerges from test results. Do stakeholders prefer charts, words, or colorful graphs? Visualizing data and insight to support audience preferences makes it easier to build understanding and buy-in.

A digital executive and his team at a top insurance carrier led a site redesign that delivered 500 percent growth in leads generated, based on pre- and post-reads. Sounds amazing, right?

The site experience team was celebrating what they saw as a big success. But the company's sales leaders had a different view. They could not see the impact in the bottom line (or in their commission checks) and as a result, withheld applause.

Of course, lots of factors affect the many sales funnel steps for an intermediated business—from completing a form to getting a call-back, having a meeting, assessing options, completing applications and underwriting, accepting the offer, making payment, and finally closing the sale. But for all practical purposes, it's a failure of the test that does not bring stakeholders along by translating results into their view of success.

And, in a sector driven by a historically stable distribution model, success in a new channel could be a threat to people whose incentives are connected to the old way of doing things.

The moral of this story: identify stakeholders and get them on board as early as possible, and always before the test is implemented and results are generated. Smart people can discount test results that cause personal discomfort. That's why building buy-in is as important as getting the design, talent, capabilities, and output reporting details right.

Where do you start and how do you move forward?

Two pieces of advice:

> **1. Think big. Start small. Act quickly.** Especially start small. Be really specific about the questions you want the tests to answer. You cannot afford to boil the ocean. Some startups succeed by going after a specific learning niche. Even global

companies start with focus on a very specific test objective, and then broaden.

2. Iterate and know when to persist. When statistical knowledge, logic, judgment, and stakeholder needs all come together the testing path will be anything but linear.

A financial institution selling a complex product initiated an experiment whose goal was to understand direct-to-consumer selling dynamics, from marketing message to application submission.

Only a small number of applications were submitted online. So the test was seen internally as a failure. But the team leading the test did not give up. They introduced econometric techniques to determine the overall business impact for the population receiving digital messaging. It turned out that among the digital message recipients, business results were measurably up. Digital communications were effective in driving incrementally more prospects to contact an advisor to seek assistance versus traditional methods. Client preference was to follow up the digital marketing message by speaking with a person, not to submit an application online.

In retrospect, this buyer journey makes a lot of sense given the nature of the product offer. Had the team not persisted to assess results more thoroughly the value of the multichannel experience would have been missed.

Testing and experimenting are pillars of scaling. There will be hiccups no matter how well designed the plan. As with the entirety of the business, the testing process itself will develop and refine with experimentation.

THREE Cs OF
TESTING AND EXPERIMENTING

Capabilities:

Visualizing the Testing and Experimenting Capability

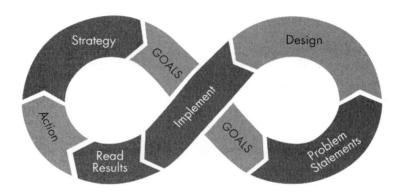

Process: An infinity loop—because each test and result leads to new questions, tests, and results.

Foundation: The business-model drivers—the design as you would like it to be, and the reality of performance

People & Environment: Diverse functional, technical skill sets, and stakeholders. Must have: operational knowledge of how the business works and what moves the levers, embracing intellectual curiosity

➤ **Inputs:**
- **Strategy**
- **Goal(s)**
- **Problem Statement(s)**

➤ **Execution:**
- **Design**
- **Implement experiments**

➤ **Learn & progress:**
- **Results**
- **Actions**

Connections:

Team structure: The Pod

In a conventional hierarchical structure, people's accountability (and incentives) align to their organizational silo (and manager). An alternative structure: create a testing team whose role is to converge around a problem statement—designing, testing, solving, and implementing—then disbanding.

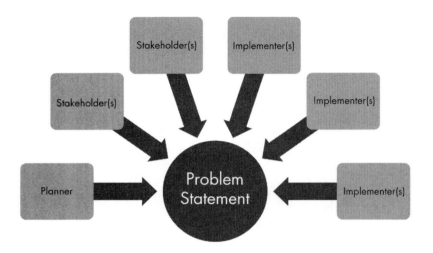

The "Pod" is a semi-permanent, virtual structure driving speed and solutions. Even if an organization is large enough to dedicate a team, a more powerful approach is to tap into people around the organization for different perspectives, specialized knowledge, and relationships.

Dedicate the implementers full-time to solve the problem statement over a sixty-to-ninety-day period. The implementers might be from analytics, product, UX/design, and channel execution. Legal or compliance should be on the team as partners in making the tests happen, not as approvers at the end of the line.

The traditional way is to assign people from each silo to assist on tests—in addition to everything else already on their plates. The risk is testing sits on the side of the desk. The Pod's value—a highly focused, get-it-done team—is not realized.

The Pod:

➤ Engages employees in development assignments where they apply expertise in new directions.

➤ Gets everyone to feel vested in answering the question.

➤ Increases objectivity about what the data is revealing, and how to push business model operating levers to act upon findings.

➤ Allows for faster decision making.

Culture:

Cultural attributes for successful testing and experimenting include:

➤ **Desiring learning** through a proactive search for knowledge and understanding.

➤ **Fearless about failure or retribution.** "Fail fast, leave it in the dust, and go on to the next thing," says Donna Peeples.

➤ **Focused on the outcome**, scaling and sustaining the business model.

➤ **Courageous and confident.** There could be little (or nothing) upon which to look back, no precedents to model. There could be an incredibly successful legacy now facing disruption.

➤ **Proactive**. Testing to push the boundaries of any orthodoxy, even the limits of policies or regulations.

➤ **Collaborative**. Engaging stakeholders whose worlds are being questioned, given test goals, and whose support is required.

➤ **Creative and thoughtful**. Imagination, dot connecting, and critical thinking animate data and lead to insight, implications, and impact.

Chapter summary

➤ Testing and experimenting depend upon willingness to explore, diverse capabilities, investment, and commitment.

➤ Effectiveness depends upon knowing the business priority, aligning learning priorities and test design to strategy, pursuing and acting upon post-testing analysis, and keeping an active inventory of tests and experiments.

➤ There is no excuse not to test and experiment.

➤ Be clear on what types of insight are needed: Hindsight— descriptive results of what happened, insights—diagnostic results explaining why something happened, or foresight— progressive insights about how to make something happen.

➤ Three guideposts for testing and experimenting: 1) defining the question, whose answer will enable better decisions, 2) understanding the business model at an operational level, and

3) anticipating execution requirements to translate findings into actions.

➤ Three pitfalls: 1) failure to connect strategy all the way through to test methodology, design, execution, interpreting results, and taking action, 2) failure to go deep enough in post-test analysis, including running iterative test cycles to answer the next set of questions, and 3) failure to maintain an inventory of tests and experiments including design, hypotheses, findings, and actions.

➤ Take full advantage of proprietary data before going to external sources. Make the ongoing investment to capture, organize, and make sense of your own customer data.

➤ A good approach to focusing test goals is to fill in the blank in the sentence: "We will be successful in our venture if _____ happens." Defining test goals and priorities at the outset enables an integrated plan that will maximize learning.

➤ As always, diverse people collaborating make the difference: data experts along with those who shape the strategy and brand, engage directly with customers, and know the wiring and plumbing of the business model. Include the skill sets of both the planner and the implementer.

➤ Testing requires infrastructure. What is good enough for early efforts? What is required to scale? Solve for the strategy, goals, and implementation.

➤ By design, tests and experiments should answer otherwise unanswerable questions. That means there could be surprise answers, disappointing answers, uncomfortable answers.

➤ Focus on what you can read and act upon. Get buy-in on the measurement standards up front—not just the types of metrics, but also the targets defining success.

➤ Iterate and persist.

CHAPTER 9

Anticipating and Adapting

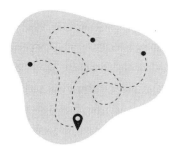

Scientists believe humans are the most adaptable species on the planet. Our capacity to adjust to changes threatening survival is why we have evolved through millennia, and why we are still here. Our brains enable us to figure out how to operate under new conditions. This ability has had a lot to do with why we manage to outlast other life-forms. Dinosaurs disappeared not because of bigger, faster, or meaner beasts coming after them. They failed to adapt.

Shift gears to the comparatively straightforward world of businesses selling products. Adapting to market conditions by making predictable, controllable, incremental moves used to be good enough. Take the examples of quick service restaurants such as McDonald's and Starbucks. Like other brands that pursued geographic expansion, these two branched out internationally as one tactic to support growth. To succeed in new places, they adapted menus, pricing, and décor to local expectations and norms.

We humans have a good track record of reacting to what is within sight and what we can believe with certainty. We adapt when the upside or downside are big enough to get us past inertia. We seek to minimize uncertainty to survive. We don't adapt to live larger.

Now, the pressure is on to adapt at high speed, and also to many concurrent changes. That is a tougher challenge, especially for people within big companies built with multilayered organizations, systems, and processes. Moving in opposition to embedded infrastructure designed to produce defined outputs can feel like walking into a gale-force wind. Our tendency to move toward safety is perfect for meeting short-term goals. And when the next few quarterly forecasts look achievable, management is slow to act upon even obvious, fact-based shifts.

Pass by a bank branch and note how few people have gone beyond the ATMs. Wonder why these institutions have not adapted more quickly and creatively to here-and-now customer experience expectations?

Slow and measured response may be okay for slow, measurable, and controllable shifts. But such a strategy puts relevance at risk when speed and unpredictability are constant, and discounts the possibility of being upended by faster new entrants with no legacy burdens.

Even the most adaptable can improve at:

➤ Embracing ambiguity, versus minimizing uncertainty

➤ Exploring the unknown for opportunity, versus seeking safety in the known

➤ Pausing to inquire and seek answers, versus rushing past questions

Psychiatrists characterize anticipation as a motivator. Anticipating is a routine activity for working through tough moments. Take that dreaded visit to the dentist. Simply by anticipating and engaging in reassuring self-talk, we manage our stress ("It won't be that bad—I'll get through it."). Anticipating stimulates positive emotions, as in how I feel anticipating a vacation scheduled months in the future.

You may be on top of your market, basking in a big win. Or maybe scaling is just within reach, having discovered, resourced and launched a growth concept. Or you may be tackling disruption as an agent of transformation. Play by this ground rule to keep your vision fresh and vibrant: Anticipate whenever you can, and get on pace to adapt when the unanticipated happens.

What to anticipate

Obvious and irrefutable trends are easy to explore thanks to discoverable, free thought leadership content, government surveys, and virtual and live events. A good network of relationships is also a great resource. Consider just these five mega-trends, all game-changers:

➤ **Demographics**: shifts in age, cultural, religious, geographic and economic cohorts affecting people's needs, habits, attitudes, and preferences.

➤ **Natural resources**: population growth and movement, climate change, and demand for resources affecting food, water, and energy quality and supply.

➤ **Individual empowerment**: reduced overall poverty (notwithstanding wealth polarization—a trend in and of itself), increasing access to education, and also to manufacturing, communications, and healthcare advances.

➤ **Dispersion of power**: the continued shift of power to networks and alliances, changing who has influence and authority.

➤ **New technologies**: both solving problems and creating consequences.

These mega-trends are seeds of massive unsolved problems and growing needs. They are sources of ideas for new ways to attack old problems. They are raw material to inspire vision and purpose.

Spotting trends brings us back to the beginnings of the Seek, Seed, Scale framework: Discovery, passion and purpose, and resourcefulness. Trends contribute to the next cycle of insights and ideas that inform evolution from what is today to what will be tomorrow. They are springboards.

Why is anticipation such a challenge?

Absent a known future, anticipating is hard. There's no appointment time—like that commitment to sit in the dentist's chair. There's no certainty of a positive end point—as in the upcoming vacation. And, especially when things are good, why bother?

Just start with a conversation exploring these questions:

➤ What can you see, sense, or deduce now to advance your purpose pursuing the next innovation, given the certainty of change?

➤ What is over the horizon that could suddenly be right here, even just months or weeks from now?

➤ How can you channel the right amount of energy into anticipating?

Neuroscience research suggests that as humans we can apply antic-ipation as a mechanism for looking ahead toward possibilities. There are just two starting points so simple they can be committed to memory and action:

1. **Recognize biases**. We all adopt assumptions that shape how we frame and control our environment. We buy into the assumptions of people we respect. We follow the lead of people whose positions suggest they know. What assumptions shape your outlook and choices? What biases influence decisions about products, customers, channels, and other aspects of innovation strategies?

2. **Be willing to question biases**. Can you recall a class, meet-ing or other group setting feeling certain participants had unasked questions? How many times have you felt that asking a question might look bad or betray your singular ignorance? School systems focus on delivering test performance. Corpo-rate meetings focus on finishing the agenda with Q&A crammed into the last few minutes. We aren't trained to ask a lot of questions, let alone question and then challenge our own assumptions and biases.

Reshaping perceptions from what *is* to what *is possible*—investing in being curious versus putting energy into maintaining the presumed safety of the status quo—the big breakthrough starts by removing self-imposed barriers.

Think about this example. One of our ancient ancestors picked up a rock. For some reason it occurred to this caveman to examine the rock, play with it, roll it around, maybe depending upon its size and shape toss it or drop it or bang it against another rock. Such simple

experiments got this curious caveman, and perhaps some of his buddies, to shift from seeing a rock as a rock, to seeing the possibility of a
rock as a tool, a weapon, or something upon which to sit. And then he
figured out that different rocks could be put to different uses. This per-
ceptual shift stimulated life-changing innovation.

Expanding needs, more complex problems, and unforeseeable
opportunities are all heading our way. We just do not yet know exactly
how, or when, or what the intensity of change will be.

Anticipate different futures to get ready.

Why are some organizations better at anticipating and adapting than others?

Businesses that reinvent have four traits in common. They:

1. Pay attention to and act upon social and economic trends.

2. Know and are passionate about their vision and purpose.

3. Engage in experimentation and value diverse perspectives.

4. Do not allow themselves to be taken hostage by an investor
agenda misaligned with vision and purpose.

How much of a factor is company size? Is the ability to anticipate
and adapt different for a startup versus a grown-up organization?
Experts on "both sides of the aisle" agree that size is an inhibitor. The
sheer complexity of processes, policies, and silo structures make large-
scale change a challenge. Take into account the biases on top of all of
the complexity, and even optimists place below-average odds on big
companies' ability to change.

Yes, there is a small club of companies whose size and scope does not burden relentless ability to take charge of the future. You know who they are: Facebook, Apple, Amazon, Netflix, Google. Leadership, vision, purpose, and culture fuel foresight and reinvention.

But in other organizations, incentives encourage moving up the ranks of a hierarchy that sustains a legacy business model. The people climbing the ladder are smart and credentialed. They use digital technologies all the time. They carry the iPhone, buy with Amazon Prime, manage more and more of their lives online, and use social media constantly. They are in the thick of disruption. How many have the skills, mindset, courage, and confidence to rewire businesses?

Don't assume that small organizations, even startups, are exempt from the challenges of anticipating and adapting. The most successful startups go through one or two pivots as they figure out their fit to the market and few are able to adapt effectively.

Enabling a team to anticipate and adapt

Distill anticipating and adapting down to decisions and behaviors. There is no silver-bullet answer (sorry!), but entrepreneurs, corporate innovators, and investors agree on where to focus. Sometimes small steps are required for gradual impact; sometimes quicker, more obvious impact is possible. Suggested tactics to boost anticipating and adapting effectiveness:

> ➤ **Goals and metrics:** Set expectations that anticipating is a valid use of effort and resources. Management teams in grown-up companies like to deliver certainty and abide by an earnings process that discourages deviation. Set the target, and hit the target. Metrics don't reward anticipation—except after the fact, when everyone takes credit for having seen the future.

Anticipation is not built into the fiscal year, and is too theoretical even for most five-year plans. An exception has been Amazon, where Jeff Bezos has set expectations, back to his first shareholder letter, about the commitment to being ahead—way ahead—even at the expense of short-term profits. You may not be tracked by Wall Street analysts, and you will unlikely be building the next Amazon, but you will need to win support for where you place effort from executives, board, and investors.

➤ **How things get done, not just what gets done.** Old methods don't work to solve new problems. As you anticipate the future, do not underestimate retooling—people, process, infrastructure, how resources are allocated, and how decisions are made. You may even need to take a step back from agile. Okay, that sounds like heresy. Agile is an incredibly powerful methodology to solve problems after they occur. It arms a team with discipline to beat out a slower rival. But it can create blind spots for anticipating and jumping ahead. Don't let devotion to agile steer the team in the direction of being overly focused on today's steps.

➤ **Enduring vision and purpose.** A founder shared a story about building a company purely with the goal of attracting VC funding and exiting. The business developed good technology, a strong value proposition, and an enviable list of clients. And in fact the exit goal was achieved. Within less than two years, the value of the exited company had gone to zero. What happened? Once sold, the company ran out of purpose. During due diligence, the buyer overlooked conflicts between its business model and that of the acquired company. Post-closing, clients questioned whose side the combined company was on. For their part, employees were saddled with either a purposeless subsidiary, or were now joined up with a company whose strategy worked against clients' interests. Employees fled, as did 80 percent of clients, who had been in exclusive relationships with the acquired business and no longer believed they could be well served.

➤ **Value people who see to the next horizon line.** Some people are simply better than others at seeing beyond what is happening today. Their specialty is taking big, nonlinear leaps. But, especially in a grown-up business, these people are perceived as dreamers who don't affect results. True, they may not be making the numbers for the quarter or the year, but they have the ability to shape the future. Be sure the anticipators have a home on the team. Provide air cover. If you are that dreamer, find an executive sponsor with the authority to be an effective advocate.

Don't expect linear results or an exact timeline. The effects of anticipating trends and adapting to change are unpredictable. Account for setbacks. Be ready to accelerate. Expect to iterate. Above all, do not lock in a precise date, hour, and minute for arrival at the next finish line. Reapply the lessons of prototyping—small steps, experimentation, and learning.

What makes some people better at transformation than others?

What is it that makes some people able to imagine a different future and create that future through leadership and action? It's a matter of who we are. Look to successful entrepreneurs for patterns and clues.

Study findings show that entrepreneurs have an internal autopilot mechanism searching for better ways to do things. They create an image of what is possible, completely different from the present, gauge whether trends enable momentum, and then they get moving.

As an example, step back to 1999, when Joshua Green established Friends of the High Line, a group of Manhattan West Siders who were able to imagine transforming abandoned railroad tracks into an elevated ecosystem. Demographic, workforce, transit, urbanization, real estate, and other factors fed public and private sector support for reinventing the site as a recreation, retail, arts, and dining destination. An urban wasteland was transformed into a dynamic residential, tourist, commercial, and corporate magnet.

Relatively few people possess such foresight. In fact, among individuals who have completed the Myers-Briggs Type Indicator assessment, slightly more than 10 percent fall into the "NT" categories where inventiveness, and abstract and conceptual thinking, are strengths.[1]

Beyond imagination and curiosity, people who excel at transformation share these traits. They:

➤ Have a true "North Star" to serve people's needs;

➤ Are able to tune out naysayers—those who see anticipators as "crazies";

➤ Possess confidence and courage to step beyond where most others can see;

➤ Partner with people who complete the bundle of creative, technical, operations, and influence skills required for execution;

➤ Sustain an attitude, outlook, and relationship network that fuel luck.

Can individuals or teams get better at anticipating and adapting? To an extent, yes, they can. Providing knowledge that increases understanding of change drivers helps, assuming a willingness to listen and learn. Affecting attitudes and changing habits are harder. To do so, seek ways to reduce resistance by those not ready to get on board, but who are open-minded. Be adept at filtering helpful insights including from resistors. The longer the distance to change, the more important for leaders, doers, and influencers to get on board—or resistance will overwhelm opportunity.

Address the emotional component of change

Every culture has idiosyncrasies and norms, and every organization has its own history, performance, and market dynamics. These elements frame whether and how people step away from today's comfort zone—be it at the water cooler or as they choose to create or inhibit change in their daily roles. Successful change makers offer tested and proven strategies:

➤ **The "rip off the Band-Aid" approach.** Chango cofounder, ad-tech executive, and entrepreneur Dax Hamman says, "When you have done the best you can, get on with it."[2] His logic: most people will ultimately get on board if they see decisiveness and consistency. Different people learn and react in their own ways, but it's safe to assume that most appreciate clear direction. Clarity dispels confusion, and people's reactions reveal the supporters, fence sitters, and resistors. Think about manager Billy Beane in the movie *Moneyball*—a pop culture example of what "ripping off the Band-Aid" looks like. He could not be clearer about expectations he has of the team—anticipating change and adapting to win.

➤ **The "leverage the potential for crisis … but do so with care" approach.** Laurel Blatchford, introduced in Chapter 6, sees potential disruption as a stimulus to innovate. The affordable-housing sector faces a rewrite of long-established government funding policies. Housing insecurity is becoming more widespread. Government policy affects private-sector participation in creating affordable housing supply. Laurel says, "People do not want to be threatened by hearing leadership say things like 'there is a crisis.' That is not a rallying cry. We want to seize the opportunity for innovation that policy disruption brings, starting with planning for what we are going to do about it." Laurel is pulling the team toward anticipating how to fulfill their mission without ringing alarm bells.

➤ **The "give them an incentive to change" approach.** Mark Walsh headed the Office of Innovation and Investment at the Small Business Administration, and has also held a variety of private sector and startup roles. He tells a story affirming his belief that most people will not adapt to a big new challenger idea without an incentive. Some years back, he started a company to crowd-source advertising creative. The goal was threefold: higher quality, wider creative talent choice, and lower cost. Not surprisingly, incumbent agencies pushed back hard on what they saw as a threat. Mark says, "What initially made no sense was that client-side brand managers, who stood to save money and get access to new creative talent, also pushed back. They saw cost savings as a threat, not an incentive. After all, the script inside their heads said, 'If I've been paying six figures for a video or commercial, and you tell me it can be created for a small fraction of what I have always paid, how does that make me look?'"

➤ **The "shrink the change" approach.** As president and chief executive officer of AICPA business unit CPA.com, Erik Asgeirsson leads technology-based programs to transform the accounting profession. Accounting services are being disrupted by technology and workforce dynamics. Erik engages members to implement innovation as a way to build their practices, rather than over-describing the enabling technologies. The key to getting buy-in, he says, is to "shrink the change."[3] This also means not everyone at once. Erik says, "Work with early adopters, get it right, focus on some niche markets, get the pragmatists to move it into the early majority and across the chasm. When we are rolling out new services we are even more measured in not trying to jump to the late majority before we get use cases and success stories. We are patient *and* act with urgency."

Can any organization change?

Not always. So many moving parts are in play. The issue is persistence to activate and coordinate the moving parts required for change. Can the retail sector adapt to Amazon's marketplace disruption? Theoretically yes, but the capital, time, talent, and culture simply may not be there. Will the banking sector reinvent itself to meet demographic, technology, experience, economics, and changing societal needs and attitudes toward saving and borrowing? It is possible to envision the blueprint, but can these institutions establish deeper trust with customers and operate with agility, while also managing risk and compliance mandates? Will the talent suited for these tasks want to join a banking organization, or will they see themselves pursuing innovation free of a legacy?

Advice to any change maker passionate about finding and delivering on what's next in their sector: Test whether the soil conditions are right for seeding. There may be a better field in which to sow. Ask these questions:

➤ Can change happen inside the mother ship? Is it more practical to fund a stand-alone effort, such as an incubator or lab? Or, is there a scrappy, in-between approach?

➤ Who is the change sponsor? Has an empowered leader committed head and heart to transformation? Is that person you? Are you ready and willing?

➤ What can be done to stimulate momentum for increased support? How might you demonstrate feasibility and impact to decision makers and influencers?

Use the planning process to encourage better soil conditions

Most organizations, however large or small, undertake a version of an annual planning process, with leaders mobilizing at a planning session.

Mobilizing around the annual plan is an opportunity to signal change, seek input and dialog, and focus management energy on innovation. Taking advantage of a planning event to generate momentum requires:

➤ **Advancing steps to be prepared.** Take the pulse of the organization relative to perceived opportunities and readiness to change. Anything from one-to-one interviews, to small group sessions, to a survey can work, depending upon learning goals and communications norms.

➤ **Confirming vision and purpose.** Are these guideposts stakeholder focused? Durable over time or running dry? Anchor expectations to the fulfillment of purpose. Be ready to convey expectations with clarity and conviction.

➤ **Focusing on trends.** Which ones will affect the business model, influence user and buyer preferences, and inspire new entrants and alternative solutions?

➤ **Translating trends and their implications into "so what's."** What might the top trends mean in terms of new concepts—product, service, offering, segment, or experience opportunities?

➤ **Tapping into expertise to inform critical thinking.** Steer away from premature efforts to build business cases and decide go/no go paths. The downside of teams great at execution, wielding advanced analytic capabilities, is pushing to decide way too early whether a concept taking aim at a developing trend should be pursued at scale or killed. How on earth do they know? Cultivate mindset, skills, and capabilities to test and experiment.

➤ **Designing low-resolution visualizations.** How might new concepts come to life? The Don Draper model popularized on the TV series *Mad Men* taught that the best way to sell an ad is to show the storyboard. Certainly the best way to get people excited about innovating is to help them by providing a visual of the future.

➤ **Prioritizing the best concepts.** The planning meeting is a beginning. The best thinking will be developed later.

➤ **Developing a ninety-day action plan.** A great wrap-up agenda item: Ask each person to write down and share commitments. Avoid the tendency to focus only on what to do to sell and build the concepts. Don't forget the change management plan, too. Address the knowledge, tools, resources, metrics, incentives, communications, and governance that a breakaway opportunity requires for its first breath of life.

THREE STORIES ABOUT THE POWER OF ANTICIPATING AND ADAPTING

What does anticipating and adapting look like in action? Consider these three stories.

Story one: Shifting norms trigger a new sector

Howard Lee is CEO of a stealth startup in the emerging cannabis sector. The legal cannabis market was worth $7.2 billion in 2016, and is anticipated to grow at an annual compound rate of 17 percent, creating more than a quarter of a million new jobs by 2020.[4]

From humble beginnings packing shipments for a mail-order company, Howard grew to take on executive assignments as a senior vice president at Disney. He went on to found Spoken.com, a cloud-based call center communications company. Howard is wired to be a change maker: vision and purpose led, persistent, curious.[5]

By Howard's telling, he learned lessons at each career stop that he is using to build a winning company in an emerging sector full of yet-to-be-determined state-level regulation, business models, product, manufacturing, and distribution strategies. How well he and his team anticipate will have everything to do with success. The lessons to which he adheres:

➤ **The best innovators bet on how to amaze users with unbeatable experience.** As a high school student, Howard paid his way as a first-generation American working in the warehouse of Early Winters, the first company to sell the Goretex brand to consumers. Founder Bill Nicolai's bet on using technology to redefine the climber and outdoorsman experience turned out to be transformative to his company and the category.

➤ **From day one, they pick and stick to one experience element on which to hang their hats.** At Netflix, Howard points out that the one element has been the immediacy of the experience. Netflix has never sold users on technology, or on the cloud. The company didn't build a cloud-based platform—Amazon's AWS provided the capability. Netflix built a disruptive business by enabling users to get what they want the moment they decide they want it. Apple bet that mobile consumption of data would be the wave of the future. Its one element was the browsing experience on mobile devices. (BlackBerry, famously and mistakenly, chose email).

➤ **They have an uncanny ability to anticipate the velocity of change.** Once they do, they manage pacing accordingly. This ability is at least as important as picking the right user experience element. Anyone can look ahead. Understanding change velocity is harder. Is it art? Science? Luck? How much is patience? How much is the ability to dial resources up and down, and then persist? Howard says, "Recently, Boeing announced they plan to recreate a software division they had in place fifteen years ago. They had the best avionics engineers in the world, and got rid of them." Achieving velocity is hard from a standing start. Too late, you lose. Too early, you can run out of cash or be diminished by naysaying.

➤ **They use data to support their experience pick.** Harnessing technology (whether built, acquired, or accessed via a partner) makes the experience happen. Howard says, "Customer experience backed up by data makes you more successful than the next guy. When I started in mail order the customer experience choices were seat of the pants. With data and technology, disruption via the customer experience has been enabled."

➤ **They assume setbacks and persist.** Anticipating and adapting—and whatever happens as a result of the steps taken in the market—are not linear or predictable. That's a truth to manage inside your head, and also with team members, employees, and investors.

Story two: Social mission + profit goals transform the borrower's experience

The daughter of two social workers, Rochelle Gorey is cofounder and CEO of SpringFour, a certified B Corporation social-impact fin-tech company. SpringFour works with financial services incumbents and startups connecting borrowers to local assistance and financial health resources, tools, and products. The company is helping the industry transform the experience of lower and middle-income borrowers who run into loan payment challenges.

Rochelle has knowledge of, and empathy for, this customer segment. She has worked on community reinvestment and housing programs at federal and local levels. In the course of a conversation with a loan-servicing manager she had her first insight behind what Spring-Four has become. She says, "This person told me that call-center employees had the ability to look at all of the foreclosure laws. So, I thought, why couldn't we also give reps information on how to refer callers to the right resources, versus steering them toward collections and foreclosure?"[6]

Rochelle says, "There is a lot of shame attached to financial problems. People who are in financial trouble may be afraid to reach out. They don't know there are legitimate, helpful resources. We saw, too often, unscrupulous actors approach them offering to 'help,' but ending up charging unnecessary fees or tricking them into taking title to their home."

Rochelle learned in her earlier roles that there are many not-for-profit organizations with resources to help the one-half of Americans living paycheck to paycheck. She says, "A car breakdown, a trip to the emergency room—you are going to pay those bills. Then you have a shortfall and you get behind on your loan. I said, 'Why don't we try to connect it all, and make sure people get the help they need when they need it?'" The need surfaces when they call their lender. The opportunity is to adapt the high-risk borrower experience so that the interaction with the financial institution becomes a way to connect to a support network that they may not otherwise find.

As part of its platform, SpringFour built and maintains a significant database of not-for-profit resources, accessible by financial institution call-center employees. Early results are promising: participating lenders have seen loan modification applications more than double, significant payment increases, and better customer perceptions of the brand.

SpringFour's approach is taking hold at financial institutions willing to transform a negative moment in the customer experience. They understand why repayment problems can happen—good customers have bad moments.

Rochelle's lessons and recommendations:

➤ **Be driven by what is best for the customer.** She says, "In SpringFour's case, we have a mission orientation *and* aim to make a profit, hence our B Corporation certification."

➤ **Have deep passion.** SpringFour happens to be mission and profit led. But Rochelle believes that even in a for-profit corporate structure there must be passion. Making money is not a passion that will drive transformation of any broad and enduring value.

➤ **Get the experts onto your team.** Rochelle says, "We have a kick-ass data team of subject-matter experts. Their expertise gives them a lens on what makes a good not-for-profit. Anyone can put together a list. But we don't want to be a Yellow

Pages directory. We are homing in on organizations that have the track record, capacity, and funding to do good."

➤ **Always anticipate what might be next.** With one-sixth of the economy going to healthcare expenditures, and as these expenses create hardship for more Americans, SpringFour is already looking toward its next horizon line.[7]

Story three: Technology disrupts accounting and professional services

At CPA.com, Erik Asgeirsson's role is to anticipate. As he says, "Technology is transforming the practice of accounting like it is transforming everything. We look at the future from the standpoint of broad patterns. What is happening with different technology capabilities? What does cloud computing mean to the profession? Artificial intelligence? Machine learning? Data analytics?"

CPA.com's North Star: To evolve the value of the CPA up the trusted adviser continuum. Moving closer to that goal starts with recognizing CPAs' strengths. They are valued for objectivity, independence, financial guidance, and expertise. They are knowledgeable about what makes clients' individual or professional financial lives tick. But their strengths are what also cause many to be cautious about change. Erik's advice:

1. **Anticipating and adapting are not optional.** His view of the accounting profession applies to any sector. If you are not looking at how to evolve, by the time you get around to it you will have lost both customers and internal top talent, since

they both will find out that there are much better solutions and opportunities available to them.

2. Think through "how," not just "what." What is the appetite for change among those whose support will effect transformation? In Erik's case, the goal is to move and influence an entire profession. The big change will likely arise out of many incremental changes.

3. Communicate and collaborate. What may seem obvious cannot be over-explained to teammates, investors, and other constituents. And the work of transformation depends upon being able to work together with different functional, sector, and expert teams, linking their diverse perspectives to find answers.

4. Make sure you have what it takes. Drive, passion, and intellectual curiosity—the traits that carry through the entire Seek, Seed, Scale journey—are mandatory to begin the next journey.

Understanding trends and their implications, talking about the strategy, or reviewing futurist reports only scratch the surface. Take a position on what these mean to your business. Gear decision-making and execution accordingly. Anticipate and adapt.

THE THREE Cs OF
ANTICIPATING AND ADAPTING

Capabilities:

Anticipating by reframing

Reframing is a way to challenge beliefs and free yourself and others to see the world differently. One of the barriers to change is that we get stuck inside the frame of how we see the world. We also get stuck inside the frame created by our biases. Follow this quick activity to help reframe, either individually or with a small team.

Allow about ninety minutes. Speed matters, so do not overwork or overcomplicate this exercise.

The walk-through of the exercise uses a specific and familiar customer experience in banking as an example. The steps:

1. Pick an orthodoxy that shapes how you approach customer experience for your enterprise today. (Or a product category, a customer segment, a sales method—whatever the opportunity space you would like to reframe.) For example: *Customers use branch ATMs to get cash and deposit checks, and these interactions are a primary element of customer engagement.*

2. Develop three statements that challenge this orthodoxy:
   - *There are no more cash or checks*
   - *There are no more branches*
   - *There are no more bank accounts*

3. Now choose one of these three challenges. You will work on your choice in the later steps of the exercise. Following the example above: *There are no more bank accounts, as we know them today. Customers control their money in their own individual accounts. They move money, and settle transactions on their own.*

4. Next it's your job to brainstorm what the transformed customer experience might be … how could it work? What's critical at this point in the exercise is to avoid:

- **Judging.** Use the language of "yes, and," not "no, but" to build on each thought.
- **Interrupting.** Don't take notes. Worst case, jot down your own quick thoughts. If you are working with a team, just talk about and build out the ideas.
- **Retreating** to the constraints of the present. At this point, the more out-to-the-edge of the envelope, the better.

You might come up with thought starters such as:

- *Offering account protection services to mitigate fraud*
- *Providing proactive advice on managing idle cash balances*
- *Integrating budgeting and cash flow management services*
- *Facilitating peer-to-peer lending by acting as a matchmaker between deposit holders and borrowers*
- *Et cetera (come up with at least 5 or 6)*

5. Now it's time to choose one concept to develop into a pitch. Follow this deliberately brief worksheet as a guide. Allow yourself thirty to forty-five minutes to complete. Put all of your focus on listening and building on each other's out-loud thoughts. Complete the worksheet when it has been fleshed out in the conversation.

Pitch Worksheet

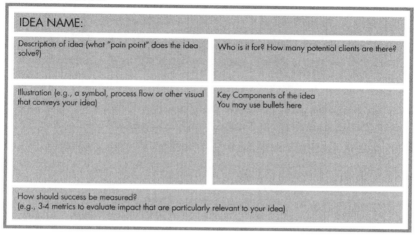

Done? You have demonstrated the ability to anticipate and generate a concept around a future that on a business-as-usual basis might be unimaginable.

Anyone can do this exercise and free themselves from the constraints of the status quo. The key at every step is to bat down judging, disrupting, or constraining ideas. Encourage the "yes, and" method of improvisational theater.

Anticipation: Keeping sight of the horizon line

Operating in the here-and-now means managing through endless details and challenges while constantly being pounded by trend forces whose outcomes are unpredictable. The possibilities can induce queasiness.

Here is a recommendation to maintain stability and focus through metaphorically choppy waters:

Sailors have a simple trick to overcome seasickness when turbulence hits. Your mom probably said it when carsickness struck on family road trips. And the same advice works for those situations where the change and ambiguity that come with complex and unexpected challenges can be unsettling.

Look at the horizon, and get some fresh air.

To face down the stress and gyrations of change that provoke unproductive behavior, encourage your team to:

➤ **Look at the horizon line** defined by how you are anticipating the future—what will be the new manifestations of your purpose. As technologies evolve, you gain insights about customers, and new needs and expectations surface. What will your success look like in twelve, eighteen, or twenty-four months as you get closer to the horizon you only see way in the distance now?

➤ **Get some fresh air** by keeping a sharp focus on what is going on around you in the world, including stepping outside the domain of "need to know." Visit your favorite museum at lunchtime. Go for a walk. Pick up a novel. Exercise. Pursue a hobby.

The message to the team: Here's what I anticipate our future will look like, on the other side of the changes we are undertaking. Sure, in the intervening time there will be variation, surprises, and ambiguity. We may feel as though we are being tossed about in a boat on rough seas, but we will get to the now-distant horizon.

Make it a habit during the routine of the daily walk around the office, and in the planned elements of your communications program, to remind people to focus on the shared view of the horizon.

Connections:

Guidelines to influence the politics of transformation

Few of us enjoy politics, but they are a reality to acknowledge and manage. Identify relationships, understand the dynamics, and recognize how you fit and where you can most effectively be positioned.

Pypestream chief customer officer Peeples keeps a checklist of influence tactics on hand. She has applied these on behalf of clients, as an AIG executive, and in her startup role.

WHAT TO DO	HOW TO DO IT
Get a seat at the table	Gauge your personal credibility. Leverage position, expertise, and connections, and use influence to be invited to a "tryout."
Understand agendas	Actively listen. Identify influencers and decision makers; spend one-to-one time to learn what's on their minds.
Know the numbers	Know the business-model drivers, the levers, risks, and opportunities. Support them in words, tone and actions.
Analyze goals & impacts	Use insights, prototyping, and data-driven learning, connecting all to business model drivers. Visualize what results might look like post-transformation.
Identify allies and resistors	Keep listening actively. Hear people out. Strengthen alliances. Win over fence-sitters, who may require individual strategies. Know when to agree to disagree, and when to engage.
Mitigate risk	Always have a Plan B on hand.
Establish credibility	Seek opinions and others' expertise, show respect for the culture and what the business has achieved, be transparent, accessible, and pragmatic.
Identify quick wins	Generate impact that may be small but eye-catching based upon business-model levers, strengths, and risks. Conduct experiments and trials to demonstrate potential.
Create coalition buy-in	Collaborate, collaborate, and collaborate. Build processes that bring people together to inform or form solutions.
Give credit	Verbally, in writing, in open forums, and online. Be authentic and generous about what and how others contribute to transformation, their sacrifices, and above and beyond effort and results.
Justify action(s)	Give people context on the what, where, why, when, and how of change. Help people understand what is happening and visualize what's in it for them.
Communicate constantly	Tell them what you are going to tell them, tell them, and tell them what you told them. Develop and implement communications strategy including lots of routine, bite-sized messaging meeting people's different communications styles,

Culture:

Defining a customer-led culture

It is hard to imagine a future for any organization unable to be customer-led. I have yet to hear an executive, ever, anyplace say they are working against the customer. But behavior and decisions tell the truth more than talk.

Here is a from/to list to grade where your organization stands. Which side of the list are you on?

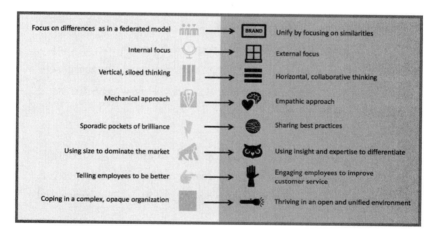

Focus on differences as in a federated model	Unify by focusing on similarities
Internal focus	External focus
Vertical, siloed thinking	Horizontal, collaborative thinking
Mechanical approach	Empathic approach
Sporadic pockets of brilliance	Sharing best practices
Using size to dominate the market	Using insight and expertise to differentiate
Telling employees to be better	Engaging employees to improve customer service
Coping in a complex, opaque organization	Thriving in an open and unified environment

Chapter summary

➤ The process of creating value and growth through innovation—led by anticipating and adapting—goes back to the beginning of the Seek, Seed, Scale framework with the new challenge of shaping what will come next.

➤ The need to innovate constantly—which is inescapable today—takes people past their comfort zones. It requires working with ambiguity versus minimizing uncertainty, exploring unknowns versus staying close to the familiar, and seeking answers versus rushing past questions.

➤ Anticipate the next horizon line by tapping into thought leadership and other relevant content available online. Five mega-trends meriting focus are: demographics, natural resources, individual empowerment, dispersion of power to networks, and new technologies.

➤ To anticipate possibilities requires 1) recognizing biases, and 2) being willing to challenge assumptions. Lowering self-limiting barriers allows the shift from seeing what *is* to seeing what *is possible*.

➤ Decisions and behaviors can move a team to be more anticipatory and adaptive. Action areas: goals and metrics, governance, process and policy driving execution, and commitment to vision and purpose.

➤ Include (and provide air cover for) team members whose specialty is seeing over the horizon. They are rare, but can turn out to be critical.

➤ The further away and more complex the transformation, the more everyone must be on board. Otherwise, resistance will overwhelm the opportunity.

➤ Address the emotional component of change. Help people to see the future, and understand their roles. You may have to rip off the Band-Aid, you may have to provide some sort of incentive, you will certainly have to "shrink the change" so people understand what is being asked of them and how they will be affected.

➤ There are common themes in the stories of other change makers: focus, leadership, speed, persistence, collaboration, vision and purpose, customer focus, passion, intellectual curiosity—a magic mix of elements that change makers have within themselves, or have the confidence and humility to learn and leverage from others.

EPILOGUE

"We are here to make a dent in the
universe. Otherwise, why else even be here."
Steve Jobs, Cofounder, Apple, Inc.[1]

We all come into the world with a purpose, born with capabilities and potential. Most people don't get to figure out what their purpose is. The business of life, making ends meet, or even just surviving take over.

You may be a member of the millennial segment, sharing student loan burdens that have surpassed the nation's aggregate credit card debt. You may be a Boomer facing the risks of living so long that healthcare costs stand to overwhelm the best-laid plans.

Chances are, though, if you have explored this book you are motivated to operate with purpose that is bottom-line plus. You enjoy the luxury of getting to figure out your purpose. You aspire to create something of value. And you have the curiosity and persistence to overcome the odds and succeed.

You are lucky, and your luck comes with a special responsibility to make a difference for others. Look around and explore. Seek insights about what gets in people's ways and how to help them. Get past cut-and-paste answers that do no more than automate an existing solution. Address needs that haven't been addressed. Plant something new that has a shot at permanence. Permanence does not need to mean forever—nowadays it is more likely a springboard that will lead to another innovation. Don't just do more of the same as yesterday or last year.

Make change happen.

Serve, don't sell.

While focused on customer segments, create value for all of the surrounding stakeholders. Do this well, and bottom-line growth and shareholder returns become byproducts. So do the impacts where the dots to financial results may be harder to connect, but are the most meaningful—strengthening the community, building workforce viability, protecting the environment, improving people's financial health.

Manufacturing and retail store jobs are on the decline in the United States. The coal industry is not coming back. With all the excitement about self-driving cars, five million people who drive for a living could lose their jobs in the next ten to twenty years.[2] Twelve percent of firms on the *Fortune* 500 list in 1955 were still there in 2016. While overall job growth is up, dislocation is affecting geographies, sectors, and demographic groups.

Economic and social stability depend upon innovation. The friction of capital and information, and the impediments that used to be caused by distance, time, and space are gone. Change makers close the gap between napkin-back idea and real-world impact.

Sacha Levy, a fellow angel investor, told an intern at his startup that there were one million reasons why the business would fail, and only one reason it would succeed.[3] That one reason would be if none of those other million reasons actually came to pass.

Reality is the list of failure possibilities is infinite and unknowable. Those possibilities exist—both real and perceived—for just about any idea that is big and bold enough to make a difference and therefore be worth realizing.

The reality is that change making is not reducible to a formula. There is no guarantee of reward, no programmable answer, even if you follow every piece of advice in this book.

Raja Rajamannar of Mastercard practices a strategic execution method that is proving effective, and is bettering the odds. He believes startup and grown-up companies bring strengths to each other that offset their respective deficits. Joining forces is a practical strategy for execution and results.

"Big companies," he says, "have funding, scale, brand, support systems, infrastructure, and budgets. But they also have bureaucracy and don't see the near-term value of innovation investments.

"Startups are hungry. They bring speed, burning passion, and agility, but they may be furiously and passionately barking up the wrong tree. They don't have infrastructure, and often lack an understanding of what it takes to scale."[4]

And, as Liza Landsman, venture capitalist and former president of Jet.com, says, "Startups don't have a monopoly on innovation, and legacy companies don't have a monopoly on bureaucracy."[5]

Magic can happen when the two work together.

There is no way to identify, let alone preempt, all failure causes. Rather, my goal has been to break down into small enough, manageable steps the things you can do to better your chances. The path is neither clear nor secure. The advantage of a book format is that it unpacks onto two planes the change maker's framework, which in reality has many dimensions. This simplification makes a better user experience for you, the reader. But, there is also the risk of the framework being perceived as simplistic.

Innovation is best illustrated as a series of irregular, interconnected, moving, and messy loops. As you pursue your purpose, pick up the pieces of supporting structure for your journey that make sense to you.

When we stand still, time is passing, and so there is less opportunity to make a difference and achieve purpose. So get moving, and while you are making your dent in the universe, give back to other change makers by sharing what has worked for you and what you have learned. With the reach and ease of social media, not sharing is inexcusable.

Make change that matters. Find your purpose and passion. Choose happiness.

ONE FINAL C—COMMITMENTS

The "start, stop, continue" exercise, also sometimes referred to as "the valentine" is here for you to take as a step toward your change making aspirations. The first step is to commit to getting started ... then to do it.

Write down the answers to the three questions.

One solid commitment in response to each question is fine—and no more than three.

Keep your commitments handy as reminders.

Share these with at least one person whom you can count on to help you stay accountable to action.

➤ START: What am I going to start doing that I know I need to be doing (up to three actions) to be a change maker?

➤ STOP: What am I going to stop doing (up to three actions) so I am not impeding my success as a change maker?

➤ CONTINUE: What am I doing well that I will continue doing to be a change maker?

ACKNOWLEDGMENTS

A colleague's request in 2010 to meet a friend of his brought Collective Intelligence founder Kevin McDermott to my office for a conversation on our shared passion—making innovation real. Likely stimulated by his deep roots in journalism, Kevin pulled out a recorder to capture our discussion. At the end, he encouraged me to write a book.

Kevin's advice became the seed not only of *The Change Maker's Playbook*. It also turned out to be the starting point for my post-corporate life: helping others with the fun, maddening, exhilarating, frustrating, and rewarding work of getting beyond the familiar to realize what is possible even when seemingly improbable to others.

My heartfelt thanks goes to Kevin for planting that seed.

At breakfast about a year before I began to write, Prosek Partners founder and CEO Jennifer Prosek suggested I try blogging as a test of my commitment to writing. That advice got me moving from zero to one. Even more valuable was her introduction to my editor Ellen Neuborne. Ellen has been with me throughout the process, generously sharing her insights, knowledge, and guidance to unpack and organize twenty-plus years of accumulated ideas running around inside my head. She mastered the challenge of keeping me on track, and always had a kind yet firm word during the harder moments of the author experience.

Nearly fifty entrepreneurs, corporate executives, private investors, and thought leaders contributed stories, lessons, advice, and content, all coming from their real-world experiences and what they have figured out about innovation.

Sincere appreciation to everyone who took my calls, engaged in interviews, and provided feedback on the work in progress: Saras

Agarwal, Erik Asgeirsson, Paul Barnett, Olu Beck, Bill Benedict, Phil Bienert, Laurel Blatchford, Greg Burns, Art Chang, Sean Charles, Geoff Chellis, David Cooperstein, Angela Curry, Joseph Fisher, Matt Foley, Steve Freiberg, Aliza Freud, Summi Gambhir, Paolo Gaudiano, Rochelle Gorey, Rick Greenberg, Gaurav Gupta, Jonathan Hakakian, Dax Hamman, Diane Hessan, Geoff Judge, Kate Kibler, Drew Lakatos, Liza Landsman, Howard Lee, Sacha Levy, Stuart Libby, Lori Marcus, Donna Peeples, Richard Quigley, Raja Rajamannar, Marian Rich, Eric Sandosham, Yuda Saydun, Jim Stikeleather, Marcia Tal, Heather Thomas, Bill Unrue, Sameer Vakil, Mark Walsh, and Ben Zombek. These individuals enriched the content of the *Playbook*. Along the way they widened my own innovation toolkit with their contributions.

I recognize that countless others influenced me since the day Steve Freiberg, then CEO at Citi Cards, tasked me with making a gigantic, proud, and successful business more innovative, putting my career on a new path. Among them are hundreds of team members, colleagues, and friends in my network who share a desire to collaborate and create a better future, support entrepreneurs, and use the tools of innovation to move forward.

Thanks to the wise advice of fellow AICPA Board Member Steve Swientozielskyj for kick-starting a peer review of the manuscript. Special appreciation as well to Jackie Stern, Phil Bienert, Matt Foley, and Dax Hamman for providing candid feedback to make this a better read for each of you. I admire these people so much, and I am honored to have worked with them and to count them as friends.

Four great professionals were with me in the home stretch. Alicia Simons helped make sense of countless launch choices. David Wilk of City Point Press shepherded the book through the editing, design, and publishing process. He also showed extreme patience with my learning curve as a newbie to an industry where author and publisher roles are being reinvented. Thanks to Jessica Berardi for creating the visual identity for the nine-step framework upon which this book is based, and to Barbara Aronica-Buck for capturing the *Playbook* spirit in a wonderful cover design.

Paul Carroll not only contributed the foreword, he also has been a friend and colleague along the way, inspiring me to be a better writer. I have valued Paul's advice and encouragement. He is a truly decent person, a great storyteller, and an accomplished author, journalist, and startup cofounder.

Finally, big hugs and endless gratitude to my family—Mitchell, Jared, Molly, and Shira—who supported me even while my research and writing took me away from them. Behind every working mom is a support system that helps keep the pieces of life together, and there is none like that provided by my family.

BRING *THE CHANGE MAKER'S PLAYBOOK* TO YOUR ORGANIZATION

➤ Any leader in any company knows they must innovate, and that there is not a set formula for doing so. The forces of change are easy to see and easy to talk about.

Knowing how to find the right opportunities and successfully bring them to fruition is hard.

Amy Radin brings the tools and advice from *The Change Maker's Playbook* to leaders across sectors and in any size organization looking to deliver business-changing innovation. Her approach will help you find the big ideas that will meaningfully impact customers and create the tangible steps to deliver in the short- and long-term for your organization.

Talk to Amy about:

➤ **The Change Maker's Keynote.** Hear Radin's nine-step framework, and use what you learn to create results starting now. Or deep dive where you want to focus most.

➤ **The Executive Closed-Door Session.** Engage a select audience in no-holds-barred conversation about how to deliver quarter-over-quarter innovation results.

➤ **The Action Workshop.** Create the deliverables you need— whether a 90-day plan for capabilities and culture change, or ready-to-test concept prototypes.

To learn more, visit AmyRadin.com or email amy@amyradin.com.

NOTES

Chapter 1

1. National Geographic News, "Flash Facts About Lightning," nationalgeographic.com, June 24, 2005.
2. Greg Burns, president, G. Burns and Associates, in discussion with author, July 15, 2016.
3. History of Heinz Ketchup Timeline, heinzketchup.com.
4. Bill Unrue, entrepreneur, Assurance CEO, in discussion with author, August 2016.
5. Raja Rajamannar, senior executive, Mastercard, in discussion with author, September 2017.
6. Matt Foley, founder, QualNow, in discussion with author, August 2016.
7. Desiderius Erasmus of Rotterdam, *Adagia*.
8. Sean Charles, cofounder, Kavyar, in discussion with author, August 2016.
9. Milton Rokeach, *The Nature of Human Values*, Free Press, New York, 1973.

Chapter 2

1. Corey Stern, "CVS and Walgreens Are Completely Dominating the US Drugstore Industry," businessinsider.com, July 30, 2015.
2. Stu Libby, CEO, ZipDrug, in discussion with author, August 2016.
3. Paul Barnett, CEO, Now What, in discussion with author, August 2016.
4. Dwayne Spradlin, "Are You Solving the Right Problem?" *Harvard Business Review*, September 2012.
5. Lori Tauber Marcus, board director, adviser, and marketing executive, in discussion with author, September 2016.

Chapter 3

1. Plato, translated by Benjamin Jowett, *The Republic*, Digireads.com Publishing, 2008
2. Centers for Disease Control and Prevention, Chart: "Unintentional Fall Death Rates, Adults 65+," cdc.gov/homeandrecreationalsafety/falls/adultfalls.html.
3. Drew Lakatos, president and CEO, ActiveProtective, in discussion with author, September 2016.
4. David Cooperstein, marketing strategist, in discussion with author, September 2016.
5. Marian Rich, improvisational theater artist, facilitator, and executive coach, in discussion with author, September 2016.
6. Lois Holzman, *Vygotsky at Work and Play*, Routledge Taylor & Francis Group, London, 2009.
7. Adobe, "State of Create Study: Global Benchmark Study on Attitudes and Beliefs About Creativity At Work, School and Home," April 2012.

Part II

1. As quoted by Theodor Dreiser, "A Photographic Talk with Edison," *Success*, February 1898.

Chapter 4

1. Walter Isaacson, "The Real Lessons of Steve Jobs," *Harvard Business Review*, April 2014.
2. Art Chang, founder, Tipping Point Partners, technology entrepreneur, and civic activist, in discussion with author, November 2016.
3. Ben Zombek, CEO, BZ Design, Inc., product design, UI/UX and marketing expert, in discussion with author, December 2016.
4. Aliza Freud, founder and CEO, SheSpeaks, in discussion with author, December 2016.
5. Sameer Vakil and Summi Ghambir, cofounders, DigiVation Digital Solutions Pvt Ltd and GlobalLinker, in discussion with author, December 2016.
6. Usability Body of Knowledge, Wizard of Oz, usabilitybok.org.

Chapter 5

1. John Reed, "Memorandum to: Messrs. Long–SVP, Kovacevich–VP, Phillips–SVP, Tozer–SVP, Re: Consumer Business," March 9, 1976.
2. Citi Turns 200: "Focus Shifts to Retail Banking," blog.citigroup.com, September 7, 2012.
3. Steve Freiberg, senior executive, adviser, and board member, in discussion with author, December 2016.
4. Diane Hessan, founder and chairman, C Space, in discussion with author, December 2016.
5. Bill Benedict, managing director, Alpine Meridian Ventures, in discussion with author, December 2016.
6. Jonathan Hakakian, cofounder, SoundBoard Angel Fund, in discussion with author, January 2017.
7. Geoff Judge, partner, iNovia Capital, angel investor, in discussion with author, January 2017.
8. Heather Thomas, CEO, Winsome and Business Builder, in discussion with author, February 2017.

Chapter 6

1. Olu Beck, CEO, Wholesome Sweeteners, in discussion with author, January 2017.
2. Mark Walsh, angel and venture investor, former head of Innovation and Investment, United States Small Business Administration, in discussion with author, February 2017.
3. Dwight D. Eisenhower, as documented in www.eisenhower.archives.gov.
4. Rick Greenberg, CEO, Kepler Group, in discussion with author, January 2017.
5. Paolo Gaudiano, founder, Aleria, and executive director, QSDI Initiative, City College of New York, in discussion with author, January 2017.
6. D. Kahneman and A. Tversky, "Prospect theory: An analysis of decision under risk," *Econometrica*, 47, 263–291, 1979.
7. Laurel Blatchford, SVP and chief program officer, Enterprise Community Partners, in discussion with author, January 2017.

8. Michael Schneider, "Google Spent 2 Years Studying 180 Teams. The Most Successful Ones Shared These 5 Traits," inc.com, July 19, 2017.

Part III
1. Teri Evans, "Creating Etsy's Handmade Marketplace," wsj.com, March 30, 2010.
2. Eugene Kim, "Salesforce CEO Marc Benioff Built a $50 Billion Empire By Following 7 Lessons From His Nemesis Larry Ellison," businessinsider.com, September 5, 2015.

Chapter 7
1. Aria Hughes, "Science of the Drop," wwd.com, June 1, 2017.
2. Ben Gilbert, "24 of the biggest failed products from the world's biggest companies," businessinsider.com, December 29, 2016.
3. Peter Thiel with Blake Masters, *Zero to One: Notes on Startups, or How to Build the Future*, Crown Publishing Group, New York 2014.
4. Brian Solis, "Are Corporate Innovation Centers the Last Hope for Companies Too Big To Fail?" innovationmanagement.se, February 9, 2017.
5. Richard Quigley, president, Cobrand Credit Card Partnerships, JPMorgan Chase & Co., in discussion with author, May 2017.
6. Jeff Bezos, founder and CEO, Amazon.com, Inc., letter to shareholders, April 12, 2017.
7. Kate Kibler, fashion industry executive, in discussion with author, May 2017.
8. Geoff Chellis, president, Expedia Consulting Group, in discussion with author, March 2017.

Chapter 8
1. Ballantine Corporation, "The History of Direct Mail Marketing," www.ballantine.com, August 14, 2014.
2. Tim Matthews, *The Professional Marketer: Everything You Need to Know But Were Never Taught*, Embarcadero Press, New York 2014.
3. Donna Peeples, chief customer officer, Pypestream, in discussion with author, July 2017.
4. Eric Sandosham, PhD, founder and partner, Red & White Consulting Partners, LLP, in discussion with author, July 2017.
5. Marcia Tal, CEO, Tal Solutions, LLC, in discussion with author, June 2017.
6. Angela Curry, president and chief operating officer, Arcuriam, LLC, in discussion with author, June 2017.

Chapter 9
1. The Myers & Briggs Foundation, 2014. Sourced during July and August 2017, http://www.myersbriggs.org.
2. Dax Hamman, partner, Reinvent Partners and Fresh Media, in discussion with the author, May 2017.
3. Erik Asgeirsson, CEO, CPA.com, in discussion with author, July 2017.
4. Deborah Chardt, "Marijuana Industry Projected to Create More Jobs Than Manufacturing by 2020," forbes.com, February 22, 2017.

5. Howard Lee, founder, Spoken Communications, in discussion with author, August 2017.

6. Rochelle Gorey, cofounder, CEO, and president, SpringFour, Inc., in discussion with author, June 2017.

7. Rosenthal, Elizabeth, "How the High Cost of Health Care Is Affecting Most Americans," NYTimes.com, December 18, 2014.

Epilogue

1. Steve Jobs, widely cited without a specific attribution, possibly *Playboy* interview in 1985.

2. Stephen Greenhouse, "Autonomous Vehicles Could Cost America 5 Million Jobs. What Are We Doing About It?" latimes.com, September 22, 2016.

3. Sacha Levy, angel investor, in correspondence with author, October 2017.

4. Raja Rajamannar, senior executive, Mastercard, in discussion with author, September 2017.

5. Liza Landsman, former president, Jet.com, in discussion with author, September 2017.

BIBLIOGRAPHY

Adobe Systems, "State of Create Study: Global Benchmark Study on Attitudes and Beliefs About Creativity At Work, School and Home," adobe.com, April 2012, accessed March 2017.

Ballantine Corporation, "The History of Direct Mail Marketing," ballantine.com, August 14, 2014, accessed June 2017.

Beals, Gerald, thomasedison.com, February 1997, accessed November 2016.

Beaton, Caroline, "4 Personality Types That Make Successful Entrepreneurs," businessinsider.com, March 30, 2016, accessed May 2017.

Bendle, Neil T., and Charan K. Bagga, "Should You Use Market Share As A Metric?" sloanreview.mit.edu, April 20, 2016, accessed July 2017.

Bevan, Nigel, Managing Editor, "Wizard of Oz," usabilitybok.org, accessed December 2016.

Bezos, Jeff, "Amazon.com, Inc., 2016 Letter to Shareholders," Amazon Investor Relations Website, April 12, 2017, accessed 9/2017.

Bill, Joe, "What Improv Can Teach Leaders About Listening," Collectivenext.com blog, September 1, 2016, accessed 10/2016.

Burrus, Daniel, "4 Ways Agility Protects the Status Quo (And 5 Reasons Anticipation Is Better)," burrus.com, May 11, 2017, accessed June 2017.

Burrus, Daniel, "Have A Business Problem? Just Skip It," fastcompany.com, January 20, 2011, accessed July 2017.

Centers for Disease Control and Prevention, Chart: Unintentional Fall Death Rates, Adults 65+, cdc.gov, accessed November 2016.

Chardt, Deborah, "Marijuana Industry Projected to Create More Jobs Than Manufacturing by 2020," forbes.com, February 22, 2017, accessed August 2017.

Citigroup, "Citi Turns 200: Focus Shifts to Retail Banking," blog.citigroup.com, September 7, 2012, accessed February 2017.

Del Rey, Jason, "This Is The Jeff Bezos Playbook For Preventing Amazon's Demise," recode.net, April 12, 2017, accessed April 2017.

Deutschman, Alan, *Change or Die: Could You Change When Change Matters Most?* New York: Harper, 2007.

Dreiser, Theodore, "A Photographic Talk with Edison: A Quiet Interview in His Laboratory; the Story of 52 Years of Magnificent Work," books.google.com, 1898, accessed November 2016.

Eisenhower, Dwight D., Eisenhower.archives.gov, accessed May 2017.

Erasmus Desiderius, *Adagia*, Joa Frobenius, Ghent University, 1523, books.google.com, digitized 2012, accessed April 2017.

Evans, Teri, "Creating Etsy's Handmade Marketplace," wsj.com, March 30, 2010, accessed February2017.

Farrokhnia, R.A., "Building Teams For A Prototyping Sprint: Learning From Google, NASA, and Other Top Organizations," Columbia Graduate School of Business Executive Education Webinars Video Library, accessed July 2017. Link: https://www8.gsb.columbia.edu/video/videos/building-teams-prototyping-sprint-learning-google-nasa-and-other-top-organizations

Gallo, Amy, "How to Get Your Idea Approved," hbr.org, November 15, 2010, accessed April 2017.

Gaur, Tim, " 6 Awesome Ways To Connect With New Employees," blog.pollevery-where.com, June 28, 2017, accessed August 2017.

Gilbert, Ben, "24 of the biggest failed products from the world's biggest companies," businessinsider.com, December 29, 2016, accessed March 2017.

Grant, Adam, *Give and Take: Why Helping Others Drives Our Success.* New York: Penguin, March 2014.

Granovetter, Mark S., "The Strength of Weak Ties," *American Journal of Sociology,* Volume 8, Issue 6, 1360–1380, May 1973, accessed September 2017.

Greenhouse, Stephen, "Autonomous Vehicles Could Cost America 5 Million Jobs. What Are We Doing About It?" latimes.com, September 22, 2016 accessed March 2017.

Grothaus, Michael, "How To Go From Idea To Prototype In One Day," fastcompany.com, May 8, 2015, accessed November 2016.

Guggenheim, Michael, "The Long History of Prototypes," limn.com, Issue Zero, 2010, accessed November 2016.

Henry, Patrick, "Why Some Startups Succeed (And Most Fail)," entrepreneur.com, February 18, 2017, accessed April 2017.

Hobcraft, Paul, "Business Model Innovation and Storytelling: How to Get The Story Right?" blog.business-model-innovation-com, March 21, 2014, accessed December 2016.

Holzman, Lois, *Vygotsky at Work and Play.* London: Routledge Taylor & Francis Group, 2009.

Hughes, Aria, "Science of the Drop," wwd.com, June 1, 2017, accessed June 2017.

Hunt, Vivian, Dennis Layton, and Sara Prince, "Why Diversity Matters," mckinsey.com, January 2015, accessed May 2017.

Ibarra, Herminia and Mark Lee Hunter, "How Leaders Create and Use Networks," *Harvard Business Review,* January 2007, accessed February 2017.

Isaacson, Walter, "The Real Lessons of Steve Jobs," *Harvard Business Review,* April 2014, accessed July 2017.

Kahneman, D., & Tversky, A., "Prospect theory: An analysis of decision under risk," *Econometrica,* 47, 263–291, 1979.

Kelley, John F., "An iterative design methodology for user-friendly natural-language office information applications," *ACM Transaction on Office Information Systems,* Volume 2, Issue 1, 6–41, 1984.

Kim, Eugene, "Salesforce CEO Marc Benioff Built a $50 Billion Empire By Following 7 Lessons From His Nemesis Larry Ellison," businessinsider.com, September 5, 2015, accessed July 2017.

King, Georgia Frances, "A Neuroscientist Explains Why We Can't See the World Objectively—And Humanity Is Better For It," *Quartz Ideas,* qz.com, May 3, 2017.

Kraft Heinz Company, the, "History of Heinz Ketchup Timeline," heinzketchup.com, accessed October 2016.

Leonard, Kelly and Tom Horton, *Yes, And: How Improvisation Reverses "No, But" Thinking and Improves Creativity and Collaboration—Lessons from The Second City.* New York: HarperCollins Publishers, 2015.

Massey, Nathaniel, "Humans May Be The Most Adaptive Species," scientificamerican.com, September 15, 2013, accessed August 2017.

Matthews, Tim, *The Professional Marketer: Everything You Need to Know But Were Never Taught*. New York: Embarcadero Press, 2014.

Myers & Briggs Foundation, the, myersbriggs.org, 2014, accessed July 2017.

National Geographic News, "Flash Facts About Lightning," nationalgeographic.com, June 24, 2005, accessed July 2017.

O'Donnell, Charlie, "Five Pitfalls of Seed Round Hiring," thisisgoingtobebig.com, January 6, 2017, accessed March 2017.

Parekh, Rupal, "Global Study: 75% of People Think They Are Not Living Up To Their Creative Potential," adage.com, April 23, 2012, accessed June 2017.

Patel, Neil, "90% of Startups Fail: Here's What You Need to Know About the 10%," forbes.com, July 16, 2015, accessed April 2016.

Peterson, Kay and David A. Kolb, *How You Learn Is How You Live*. Oakland, California: Berrett-Koehler Publishers, 2017.

Plato, translated by Benjamin Jowett, *The Republic*, Digireads.com Publishing, 2008, accessed May 2017.

Prevost, Shelley, "5 Reasons Why Most People Never Discover Their Purpose," inc.com, August 29, 2013, accessed November 2016.

Reed, John S. "Memorandum to: Messrs. Long–SVP, Kovacevich–VP, Phillips–SVP, Tozer–SVP, Re: Consumer Business," March 9, 1976.

Rokeach, Milton, *The Nature of Human Values*. New York: Free Press, 1973.

Rosenthal, Elizabeth, "How The High Cost Of Healthcare Is Affecting Most Americans," nytimes.com, December 18, 2014, accessed June 2017.

Rozovsky, Julian, "The Five Keys To A Successful Google Team," rework.google.com, November 17, 2015, accessed July 2017.

Schneider, Joan and Julie Hall, "Why Most Product Launches Fail," *Harvard Business Review*, April 2011, accessed January 2017.

Schneider, Michael, "Google Spent 2 Years Studying 180 Teams. The Most Successful Ones Shared These 5 Traits," inc.com, July 19, 2017.

Solis, Brian, "Are Corporate Innovation Centers the Last Hope for Companies Too Big To Fail?" innovationmanagement.se, February 9, 2017, accessed October 2017.

Spradlin, Dwayne, "Are You Solving the Right Problem?" *Harvard Business Review*, November 2012.

Stern, Corey, "CVS and Walgreens Are Completely Dominating the US Drugstore Industry," businessinsider.com, July 30, 2015, accessed October 2016.

Thiel, Peter with Blake Masters, *Zero to One: Notes on Startups, or How to Build the Future*. New York: Crown Publishing Group, 2014.

Thompson, Derek, "What In The World Is Causing the Retail Meltdown of 2017?" theatlantic.com, April 10, 2017, accessed June 2017.

Woods, Tim, "Peter Thiel's 7 Questions for Product Innovation," blog.hype innovation.com, January 12, 2015, accessed April 2017.

Wunker, Stephen, "5 Strategies Big Businesses Use to Build A Culture of Innovation," forbes.com, July 29, 2015, accessed May 2017.

Vanderkam, Laura, "How to Get the Green Light For Your Big Idea," fastcompany.com, July 8, 2014, accessed May 2017.

SEEK

1 Discover

2 Position With Purpose

3 Be Resourceful

SEED

4 Prototype

5 Create the Business Model

6 The Green Light Moment

7 Launch

SCALE

8 Test and Experiment

9 Anticipate and Adapt

Achieve Impact

CAPABILITIES

CONNECTIONS

CULTURE